GOD KILLS

Spirituality of a
Christian Pragmatist

Library of Congress Control Number:
2014930564

Printed in the United States of America
First Edition
10 9 8 7 6 5 4 3 2 1

Cover design by Iain Morris
Interior book design by Amy Wheless

Distributed by
Publishers Group West
1700 Fourth Street, Berkeley CA 94710
Phone 510.809.3700
pgw.com

 Roundtree Press

6 Petaluma Blvd. North, Suite B-6
Petaluma, CA 94952
roundtreepress.com

ISBN: 9781937359645

CONTENTS

DEDICATION & APPRECIATION

This book is dedicated to my late parents, Art Sr. and Carol Greco—both of whom wondered why it was that every time God provided for me, it ended up costing *them* money.

Thank you. If I can be half the parent to my children that you were to Susan, Lenny, and me, I'll consider it a success far beyond anything I could ever have imagined possible.

I'm aware that my life is lived "on the shoulders" of people who have invested in it, contributing in more ways than I know. Special thanks for anything worthwhile in this project go to: clinical depression and the deep struggles that go with it; my wife, Brenda, and our children, David, Josh, and Becca, who refused to let that depression swallow me whole; the churches I've served while thinking through and discovering some important things—especially Tigard Covenant Church, who got less than they deserved from their then–crippled pastor; Fathers Thomas Brendley and Christopher Martin; Lenny and Susan; Lee Toms; Ted and Randy; Tadd, who was in my youth group in the late 70s and never forgot me; Martha and Allie; Chris, who is the only publisher I spoke with who was willing to publish this with its original title; Gary, who insisted that I do graduate work in Christian Spirituality, then made that pursuit possible; and Garth, who told me that this project would be a waste of time unless I included a chapter on celibacy.

PREFACE

Making Sense of Such a Disturbing Title

A ctually, the idea that "God Kills" is a redemptive and hopeful one. Let me illustrate by beginning this book with a shocking admission: **My life is one spent in service to an executioner king.** That's because I'm discovering that God kills and his opponent, the Devil, gives life. Now having written that, I feel compelled to go out of my way to make it clear that I actually believe what I've just stated— because I do, you see. I do believe that God is in the business of bringing death and Satan is in the business of sustaining life.

A teaser statement to get you to read on? Okay, sure, sort of, but that statement is more than just a writer's "shock-jockey" trick. For in some ways it's actually true.

Scripture, some would say, puts down such a wild statement with very little effort and in several different places. Perhaps the most obvious of these is Christ's claim in John 10 that the thief comes only to steal, kill, and destroy but that he [Jesus] came to give life, and not just *any* life, but abundant life. I wholeheartedly agree, but I do that while at the same time maintaining my original assertion: God kills and the Devil gives life. It's just that God seeks to kill what should die in us and Satan tries to breathe life into what should not be allowed to live. In other words, the abundant life Jesus comes to give is realized by means of a series of funerals over which he presides, while the "killing and stealing" of the enemy of God is done through his attempts to enliven the very beliefs, practices, and urges that have always and only served to poison us.

Ironic? Absolutely. The author of death tries to keep death alive by offering life support to the very things that will guarantee our current and eternal demise, while the giver of life brings that life about by means of a series of killings—some of which are quite brutal and all of which require us to be accomplices, as though we were participating in a string of divinely assisted suicides. Still unconvinced? Let me try to explain through story—some of my own story, actually. Even though this particular example is sort of "everyday" and not very dramatic.

I am a pastor, a quivering bundle of insecurities wrapped in thin skin, in my case. Frankly, I sometimes doubt that God has ever called a more ill-equipped person to this most precious, strategic, and honorable office. Just recently I was talking with a friend about how I felt as though God had designed me for 110 volts, then called me to a position that ran 220 through already inadequate and fragile wires. But that's for another book. For now, let me get back to my story of life and death.

As a pastor I am given daily opportunities to be too impressed with my successes and too dismantled by my failures. I'm embarrassed to say it, but I take full advantage of each of those opportunities. But I'm not the only one who uses these moments. Both have also proven to be chances for God to kill and Satan to give life. For instance: Though I'm not nearly as enamored with my own preaching as I used to be, I was successful one Sunday morning with my sermonic offering. I felt as though God had empowered what I said. The feedback I got from people who wouldn't usually say anything only helped to confirm that I had succeeded in letting Him speak through me, and right away I felt something coming alive. "I still have it," I thought to myself. "I'm a good preacher—maybe even as good as John Wenrich, Brenda Salter McNeal, or even Efrem

Smith!" I must say that I felt quite alive after that first of our Sunday gatherings, as though I wanted to yell at top volume, "I preached! Therefore I am!" Something or someone was breathing life into what I was feeling and I liked it very much. There was an immediate power surge to my ego as a familiar appetite for recognition began to insist that it be satisfied. *Dwell here*, I thought. *Milk this.*

However, it didn't take too long before that still, small voice in my head (you know, the one that always seems to come to curtail our most base enjoyments) began to whisper to me. "What is this that you are feeling?" I thought to myself, convinced that God was actually the one implanting those thoughts. "I suppose you can call it some sort of celebration of *My* work and the Spirit's gifts in you, but we both know it's nothing nearly so honorable as that." And the corrective thoughts were just that—correct. That thing into which Satan wanted to breathe life (with plenty of help from me, by the way) was something that didn't deserve to live at all. It was nothing more than the same old, sick hunger to be celebrated that had always haunted me. It was an "impulse that needed to die," and I was fairly certain God wanted to shoot it straight through the heart.

My prayer was pretty honest. "Please, Lord. That's the only thing that has even come close to feeling like life all week. Can't I at least *feel* alive? Can't I feast on this carcass of pride, just for today, just for this morning? I mean, it's not like we're talking about stealing or cheating here. This is the verbal presentation of the Bible I'm enjoying. It's a decent sermon that has me feeling so good about myself."

I sensed His answer, and it was just as honest: "Only if you're really intent on joining it as just another useless carcass. Don't you remember your own definition of humility? 'Humility is the willingness to be perceived as insignificant in order to be effective.' You preached that too. You want something that feels like life? Well, in My way of seeing things, it's self-denial and death that feels most like life. And I want to take you there. Offer this so-called 'life giver' to Me so I might slaughter it, or at least this manifestation of it."

I felt like the new student who had finally started dating a pretty girl, only to discover her family was being transferred to South America. Not all that sure that I really meant what I prayed, I at least forced out the words, issued the command— "Kill it, then, if you must. Kill it before I change my mind and completely indulge it. But don't just wound it. Every time that thing gets wounded it seems to heal up and come back even stronger than before. Kill it! And 'kill it good,' or leave it alone and let it go on seducing me! But don't just wound it!"

Then I made my way into our auditorium to get ready for the next service, smiling, shaking well-intentioned hands, and greeting folks along the way. "Yes. Hi. How are you? You did? Oh, thank you. I enjoyed preaching it too . . ." And oh boy, did I ever enjoy preaching it—but for all the wrong reasons.

I have no idea why it's so difficult for me to experience it, since it's a major theme in the life of Christ, but, like just about every major faith, Christianity is a religion of death. It's a death, however, that brings life. It's a religion of perceived weakness, but it's a weakness that proves true strength. This is the faith of dirty feet, missing teeth, swollen eyes, torn flesh, bloody wrists, splinter-filled shoulders and spear-pierced hearts. To be a

Christian is to begin a "Golgotha trek" that results in a publicly embarrassing display that looks a lot like a very bloody defeat but is actually the gateway to real life, full life, abundant life.

I am discovering that God kills and the Devil gives life—that Christ is in the business of destroying and Satan is in the business of sustaining. It's just that God seeks to *kill* what should not be allowed to live in us and Satan tries to *breathe life* into it. Perhaps that's why I find myself addressing God in a rather strange way when I pray lately. "Lord," "Savior," and "Father" are all wonderful names by which a Christian might refer to God in prayer. But recently I've been praying to him using a much less common title, his dominant title in a dying man's life:

"Oh dear Holy Assassin: Be loving enough to eliminate what pollutes my heart and erodes my soul. And when the day comes that I attempt to annul this contract, to withdraw the permission I now give, listen instead to the instructions of Your own headstrong mercy. Swallow hard, breathe deep, take aim, and pull trigger. Amen."

Theologically astute friends are right to remind me that the book's title isn't the only thing about it that's potentially bothersome. Some of the definitions I present in this work are, they insist, questionable . . . creative at best. Others, they argue the limits of orthodoxy itself. But that's not really much of a surprise, since some of those definitions (specifically the ones offered in the chapters entitled "Faith," "Yieldedness,"

"Courage," and "Humility") were born during a season in my life that might best be described by the phrase "kissing a buzz saw." Let me explain by sharing a bit from that season:

My early years as a church planter[1] were murky and foreboding. It became increasingly clear that, professionally speaking, I was likely to realize very little of what I had once considered sure and certain. I'd gotten married, completed the unofficial and virtually unpaid "apprenticeships" young pastors serve in preparation for a life in "the ministry," finished college and graduate school (with the standard burden of substantial student loans), and, some of the stories that await you in the coming pages notwithstanding, even managed to be a reasonably decent father to three children along the way.

I had eaten life's vegetables first and now it was time to enjoy its desserts. But in my case, there was to *be* no dessert. In fact, it wasn't long before it started to feel as though I was more of the *eaten* than the eater of anything, like I was a wounded, bleeding baby seal and life was an ocean full of hungry great whites on "Shark Week."

It all started one day on the way home from the office for a quick lunch. As my blue Mazda 626 rolled to a stop at a very familiar traffic signal, I had no idea that, in mere moments, a mental tornado was destined to touch down in my head. My only thoughts concerned the hour I had to eat and the chance to watch the Cubs on cable while I did so.

The corner of Highway 99 and McDonald Street was one I'd seen hundreds of times. It had one of those lights that always seemed to be red—especially when I was on my way home from the office after a particularly tiring day or in a real hurry to get somewhere. This day was no different. As I sat first in line at the signal, I noticed the Elmer's Restaurant on the left, a favorite Sunday brunch eatery for many of the families in our church, and the Union Gas Station, which had served customers for years, occupying its place on the right. Everything around me looked familiar—and it should have, since I lived only blocks away and traveled that same route many times each week.

But that day something bizarre happened to me at that corner. I arrived at the red light feeling fairly normal. I had grown used to feeling "stressed," assuming it was just a necessary byproduct of the life of a church planter. My chest felt like it was in a vise, my head felt heavy with pressure (but without the sharp pain of a headache), and I was a little dizzy—all sensations I had grown accustomed to over the years. That *bizarre something* came on quickly, as quickly as if my senses were a slideshow and someone had just pushed the button and changed the picture. For as suddenly as a person exhales an old breath and takes in a new one, nothing looked familiar to me at all. I didn't know where I was, where I was going, or where I had been. I just sat there, dazed, until the sports car behind me honked and startled me into creeping forward through the now foreign light that had turned from red to green.

As I motored slowly down the highway, a vacant reasoning process began in my head: *I'll just keep driving until something looks familiar. I think I live close to here.* It was the same sensation you get when, having visited someplace in a strange city just once, you return ten years later and try to locate it again relying solely on memory. Things seem familiar enough to keep searching, but not quite familiar enough to ever get your bearings. I turned left because it "felt" correct, then left again for the same reason. I suspected that one of the houses on the block was mine, but I wasn't sure which one. *I'll push the button of the garage door opener,* I thought. *Wherever a garage door opens, that must be my house.*

Having settled all doubt, I parked in the driveway of the house with the opening door and walked into the garage. Convinced my career (and maybe even my life) was over because of some debilitating medical condition, I sat on the garage work bench for hours and just stared at the wall as my head began to clear.

All of this happened in the spring of 1991, and I did eventually seek medical counsel. After secretly visiting one of the HMO physicians in our medical program for an initial exam, I went to a better-known doctor for a second opinion. He concurred with the first doc's diagnosis but was a bit more explicit and blunt in the way he communicated it to me. "Your experience was not the result of any sort of tumor or stroke; everything you went through on that day was the result of plain old stress and depression." Then, going on to put things more plainly in case I had misunderstood, he simply said, "In short, you snapped. Your brain is fried. Your mental and emotional knees have buckled. Do you understand?"

I was numb, but I nodded as though fully aware of what he was saying. What he said next, though, was like iced tea being poured on the back of a sleeping sunbather. "I recommend you find a different line of work," he said in an uncharacteristically severe tone. "If you won't, and, knowing you, I suspect as much, you need to get entirely away from the church—*any* church— for a minimum of six months. If you can't at least do that, chances are you'll never pastor again. And that's not even the worst-case scenario."

His advice was dead on. It was time for me to take a significant break from diagnosing the spiritual brokenness of others in order to spend some time working on my own chips, cracks, and dents. Good thing I did, too, for it turns out that I was much more compromised than anyone had realized.

Normally an off-the-charts extrovert, I had begun to dread the days when I had to be around people, choosing instead to stay in the backyard and work in the garden alone. I certainly would not have won any awards for being husband or father of the year in those days. I was short, angry, reclusive, and at times downright mean to a wife who had never been anything but sacrificially supportive. Our three young children felt it, too. I doubt they had any way to interpret what they were experiencing except to conclude that some sort of nightmare had begun that just might haunt the rest of their lives.

I felt guilty, powerless, vulnerable, and embarrassed—like someone who had spent his entire life savings to buy his dream home, only to discover after moving in that it had no interior walls. My wife had been dragged through two degree programs, worked far too hard to help finance them, agreed to move our children away from the joy and help of our families, and supported me as I turned down a secure position that would have taken us back to California (and those families) in favor of a relatively risky opportunity to start a new church. Why? Because I was convinced that success was ours for the taking.

And what did I have to show for all that youthful exuberance and hard work? A scrambled brain, a crippled soul, and a tarnished reputation. I had been diagnosed with clinical depression—the classic pastoral limp. And no one wants to leave their wagon hitched to a horse that limps.

It was while drenched in the spillage of that bucket of poison that I began to wonder what success really was. What did mature spirituality really look like—not in the well-established sense of classic theology, but in the everyday working world of tests and measures? When life requires you to fit five pounds of coffee into a four-pound can, when it feels like you're being hugged by a porcupine, when it seems as though God has been underperforming for you—what do things like faith, courage, and yieldedness look like *then*? How is success measured and defined *then*?

That's the kind of craziness I was facing when I began to question the depth of my spirituality and, most importantly, whether I really had any. And if I found that I *did*, how could I really know? It was while asking those kinds of questions, in the context of a depression so severe that at one point I actually had to make a list of reasons I should stay alive, and then ask friends to keep close tabs on me in order to minimize the chances that I would take my own life, that I came to some of the conclusions and considerations offered and intimated in these chapters.

So as you move through this book, remember that you're reading what I would consider "survival-mode lessons." These are the ideas and words of someone who had bought into a measurement of spiritual success that ultimately proved to be bankrupt, promising much but delivering little. It had turned out to be "all bag, no chips"—a meal heavy on the chewing but light on the nourishment. The "spirituality" I had adopted for myself consisted of little more than a few major rules that were, I eventually realized, kept so that I could "succeed" as a Christian without being forced to think deep thoughts. They allowed me to "follow Jesus" without forcing me to struggle with what I heard from him or submit myself to the masterful instruction of theological confusion or emotional angst. In fact, my spiritual practices served more to insulate me from those things than to teach me anything by means of them, for in that failed system of thinking, confusion and angst were actually considered *UN*spiritual.

Don't get me wrong. Depression is a horror film no one should have to see. But for me, it was also a salvation of sorts. Out of it came the realization that the safety net of my morality had a rip in it, and that tear was widening by the day. There had to be more to a bold relationship with God than what I had been propping up, and I either wanted it, or I wanted out.

My "search," which was honestly little more than a frantic, self-absorbed survival attempt at first, eventually brought me to an extended time of reflection around a single "prayer question:" "I know how the American Church defines spiritual success, God. But how do *You* define it? How is it measured in 'Heaven'?"

With that question came some reasonable demands of God, too. One of them—and I still think it was the most reasonable of all—was my insistence on answers that made common sense; that they be pragmatic. "Don't give me platitudes, please. I don't need 'floating concepts' that can't be grasped. I get enough of those from my friends and neighbors. Simplistic excitations like,'Read your Bible more' aren't helping me. I need to know what 'faith' really is, how it really works, what it looks like when it's actually pounding nails and turning wrenches. I'm asking for definitions by which I'll be able to test myself—challenges and measures that contribute to real transformation, not just surface-level behavior modification."

For a month I did virtually nothing except pray, read, think, and reflect on my big question. I don't remember exactly when, but at some point during that process I came to the conclusion that somewhere along the line I had discarded true spirituality in favor of its avatar. I'd been dancing with a corpse, then wondering why in the world the only result was that I felt more exhausted at the end of every song. What I had taken as the marks of spiritual royalty (and, therefore, things worthy of pursuit) had actually turned out to be well-dressed time bandits. I had followed them with unquestioned loyalty only to realize that, like slick hustlers in a traveling carnival, they had tricked me out of precious years I would never get back, then loaded their trucks and left in the middle of the night. All that was left was a memory, a few holes in the pavement, and a parking lot full of litter—a LOT of litter. It was time to quit flirting with this fantasy spirituality and find, then re-engage with, the real thing. The "spirituality" I thought had been giving me life was actually contributing to my slow death, and it was time for it to be forever silenced—exposed as a target to a God who kills what has no right to live but resurrects what should never have died.

This quest took me to the only place I was sure anything approaching real, authentic spirituality actually existed: it took me to yesterday, where I remembered seeing steadiness of heart and soul. It took me to "the greatest generation" and "the greatest stories of the Bible." I went to my "grandparents" and my "theological parents"—which is also to say, sadly, I went to my trash can, for that's where I, along with so many in my generation of leaders, had tossed what yesterday had tried to teach us about where to place the decimal point when it comes to real spiritual might.

And you know what I discovered as I rummaged through those garbage pails? I found brokenness, and gentleness, and contentment there; I found humility, and teachability, and yieldedness. I discovered that what on the street might be referred refer to as "kick-ass" spirituality, the kind that actually removes what needs to be removed and sustains what needs to be sustained, resides in traits that, at least by modern standards, don't (at first) appear to be very "kick-ass" at all. In fact, there was one thing every example I uncovered had in common, and it certainly didn't look muscular or dominant. Know what it was? DEATH. But this wasn't the kind of death we grieve. This was a death that made real spiritual life possible. This was the pulling of weeds in order to have the planting of a garden; it was the cutting away of rotten wood in order to have the installation of solid new timber.

This book is about those traits and that death. And it's written in hopes that at least a few who read it will decide to choose them over any alternate measure of spirituality being proposed today. For, in spite of the fact that those substitutes may be easier to obtain and simpler to manage, in my experience they are fast trains to washed-out bridges.

INTRODUCTION

A s I've already suggested in the preface, it seems to me that an awful lot that's valuable gets inadvertently thrown out with the trash these days—especially stuff that pertains to the human quest for religious sanity and healthy spirituality.

It reminds me of my childhood living room on late Christmas mornings. Christmas always started just a little bit early in my childhood home, with our family gathered around the tree late on Christmas Eve night for our favorite get-together of the year. It was time to open gifts and, like most kids, we were efficient and dutiful participants. It wasn't long before paper was flying and presents were being compared. That done, we would begin the reluctant retreat to our beds to do the impossible: go to sleep.

When the sun rose later that morning, our living room always resembled the widespread carnage after a vast and violent conflict. The discarded carcasses of gift boxes that had once rested peacefully beneath a slowly withering tree were scattered wall to wall, like so many bodies in a field the morning after a deadly battle. They had slept quietly under our tree for weeks, disguising themselves as brightly wrapped decorations. But though we had pretended to be impressed by the gift wrap, my siblings and I had really been interested in only one thing: ripping off the fancy coverings to see what was hidden inside. The morning after we had finally been allowed to do so, we would creep back down the hallway, leaving our bedrooms with a groggy fear that the gift-opening frenzy we remembered from the previous night had been little more than a cruel dream. The beautiful mess we found always proved that it had happened just as we recalled it. There was paper and disorder everywhere; the only thing that distinguished our front room from the local garbage dump on those mornings, aside from the absence of toxic, choking fumes, was that there were no seagulls or crows circling the litter.

Stacked off to the side of all that had been deemed unnecessary and therefore disposable would be three neatly placed heaps of toys and clothes. The piles were always the same height (something my parents made sure of but that I never really understood until I had children of my own) and arranged so as to ensure that nothing would be lost or forgotten. Oblivious to the mountains of irrelevant trash around us, each of us (I grew up with a younger sister and brother) would be drawn to our own cache of gifts like homing pigeons to their most familiar and comfortable perches.

Last night had not been imagined, we would slowly realize. It had been no dream. It had really happened. We had scored, and the loot of which we had taken possession *then* was ours to be enjoyed *now*. In the earliest moments of that Christmas morning (always 12:01 in our home), our parents had finally invited us to come and open the packages that had been teasing and seducing us daily from the base of the Christmas tree. It had been payback time ... time to conquer, time to grab, rip, toss, apprehend, and enjoy. And the chaotic spray of litter that the new day found awaiting it in the living room was evidence that testified to the fact that this was exactly what we had done.

One particular Christmas we had received packages from a faraway country we had only heard of on the news and about which we knew very little. The gifts were from an aunt who eventually became a beloved friend, but one we knew only by reputation when we were kids. She worked for the government and was stationed in a place called Vietnam. These gifts, our mom and dad were careful to remind us, had traveled from the other side of the world in order to sit under our tree. Because of that, they were special. We were appropriately impressed.

It was about halfway through our midnight gift-opening ritual that we tore through our aunt's brick-sized bundles. We must have looked like hungry men ripping open free lunches. Certainly something that had been shipped with such care from so far away had to be of significant value. We dug in for the feast.

Whenever gifts are involved, kids very quickly learn the art of being politely disappointed—especially when the spectacular thing they imagined is trumped by the frumpy thing they discover. The minute our exotic-looking boxes were ripped apart, all three of us knew that this was one of those times we'd need to employ those skills and fake excitement. For instead of the hidden treasure we had pictured in our minds, each box contained a simple wooden carving of an elephant, some strange-smelling packaging, and a note explaining some of the differences between African elephants and these Asian examples that still ran wild in parts of Vietnam. We were pleased but generally unimpressed with the elephants, moving on to our next conquests a bit too quickly for our parents' liking.

The next morning, after our folks had helped us gather up the mess and burn the massive pile of wrapping paper, we stopped to take more careful inventory of our booty. When it was the elephants' turn, one of my siblings noticed that each carving had strange, unexplainable holes drilled into the cheeks on either side of the animal's trunk.

"What are these holes for, Mom?" one of us asked.

"Well, that's where you put the most valuable part of the gift," she responded. "Hand me the little white tusks." Sadly, restrictions on the sale of it had not yet been put into place back then, so they were made of real ivory.

As though on cue, each of us looked to our stacks of presents, then at each other, and finally to the now raging fire. Our hearts sank—along, I'm sure, with our mom's as we realized that we had not bothered to double-check that morning's trash for any of last night's treasures. And now that "trash" was being turned to ashes in our fireplace. We had unwittingly treated as valueless and thrown away the most costly parts of what our aunt had sent. What we were left with was good, but it had been separated from what would have made it spectacular.

Suffice it to say that the idea of a contemporary church raging her way through new ideas about spirituality at the speed of light while quieter yet more valuable concepts rest in the rubble, waiting for an opportunity to transform the mundane into the marvelous, leaves me with the unmistakable taste of bile in my mouth. Besides, in my experience, most of the profundity that has blown me away spiritually turns out to have been "discovered" long (sometimes centuries) before I was even born.

So this is a book about resisting the assumption that something is better just because it's newer. It's a book that seeks to celebrate and encourage the practice of rummaging. It's an intentional trip to the dumpster to sift through the garbage in search of a five-star meal for the soul—to make sure the ivory tusks don't get pitched with the cardboard boxes. It's about rescuing yesterday's spiritual treasures from today's trash.

But sadness over the things we throw away wasn't the only catalyst for this volume. Another motivation came from the wounds of that season of depression I mentioned earlier. During those awful months of fog, I began to dwell more specifically on how unhelpful the catchy spiritualized phrases I already noted in the preface were when launched in response to real pain. "Just give it over to God" and "Have faith," were, as I said, two I heard often, but by far the most heart-wrenching of all was one particular message that came in various forms: "God must really have something great in store for you to have given you this challenge." This was a "consolation" that left me even more troubled than I was before I heard it, causing me to expand on the questions God had already been hearing from me. "Just what do those things mean, anyway? How do we gauge our level of surrender, measure our faith? How do we find out where we are on the timeline of a difficult thing passing? And come to think of it, how many other phrases and concepts that sound like spiritual depth are we throwing around with little or no understanding of what they actually even mean, not to mention how much they hurt the people who hear them?" So, pragmatist that I am, I started to search for workable, measurable definitions for some of what I now call Christianity's "celebrity phrases." They are the Khloé, Kim, and Kourtney Kardashians of Christian verbiage: famous not so much for their accomplishments as for simply being famous. And I decided it might be very helpful to change that.

As you progress through this book (should you choose to

keep reading), you'll see an attempt to take concepts that are marks of a truly mighty spirituality and assign them definitions that, though perhaps a stretch in the opinions of more careful theologians, are presented in ways that might be understood and applied at some working level. Don't overthink those definitions; they are, by design, more art than science. My intention is that, through them, people might find hope, help, and an invitation to be more like the men and women we dream of being in life's endeavor.

Because of my alignment with Christianity and my appreciation for the Bible, I spend a bit of time unpacking biblical texts in some of the chapters—certainly more than some readers would prefer and less than others need. Even when reading them myself, I began to experience a bit of mental drift—okay, I started to get a bit bored.

This is way too basic. Everyone will already know this, or, *This is far too involved. Who in their right mind would keep reading at this point?* were common thoughts during my writing and rewriting process. My encouragement is this: since you have already paid for it, you might as well finish the book. But when you grow tired of my biblical rabbit trails or are underwhelmed by the points I'm trying to make using biblical examples (perhaps because you don't share my worldview of theological convictions), just focus on the definitions and how they might be employed in your life. Those are the heart of what I'm trying to communicate anyway.

In my opinion, there is a big difference between true spirituality and the kinds of things that are often linked to it—things like power, advancement, theological pedigree, and even celebrity. That difference becomes pretty glaring when we consider some of the words that will be used to describe some of spirituality's attributes in this work—words like "humility," "yieldedness," "celibacy," and "teachability." But it's in those things, and not their cheap but more impressive-sounding substitutes, that true spiritual vigor is found. Volume must never be mistaken for depth. It's not the most articulate proponent of God who has the more developed spirituality, but the most humble. It isn't the person who can recite the greatest number of facts about the Bible who is closest to Him, but the person who is forever aware of how much remains to be learned, how hungry he or she is to learn it, and how willing he or she is to turn away from what needs to be laid to rest in order for any of that to happen.

One last request: As you turn these pages, please keep in mind the title of the first chapter and remember that there is a difference—sometimes a *BIG* difference—between the spirituality for which I hunger and the spirituality for which I occasionally settle. In other words, the fact that these thoughts have been written and published should in no way imply that they have been found and conquered, at least not by me.

I'm just sayin'...

NOTES

CHAPTER ONE
THE AUTHOR IS A HYPOCRITE

Once you read this opening chapter, you'll have to agree with its embarrassing admission: The author is a hypocrite!

THE AUTHOR IS A HYPOCRITE

My wife Brenda thinks I should be more discreet when telling stories—especially the ones where I tell on myself. "People are going to get the idea that all you ever do is mess up," she cautions, "that you are preaching one thing but living another; that you're some sort of hypocrite." Even though it's never in my best interest to do it, I'm going to ignore her. Though it makes Brenda cringe at times, I'm going to use personal examples to prove the claim made in the title of this chapter. These are personal stories of inconsistency—painful samples of a difference between what I report to believe (and still actually *do* believe) and seem to practice. They're illustrations of the slide that sometimes happens when I, for whatever reason, quit paying attention to details.

Once you read this opening chapter, you'll have to agree with its embarrassing admission: The author is a hypocrite!

"Hypocrite" is probably too strong a word, since it has to do with intent as well as practice. I never consciously intend to say one thing and practice another. But I'm aware of a nagging inconsistency that too often shows up in the life I'm rehearsing as a follower of Jesus. In fact, if "hypocrisy" seems like too strong a word, "inconsistency" feels as though it's not quite strong enough. Somewhere between those two is where I often find myself lingering for days. It's important to me that people reading this book remember that. For even if my wife, who was quite uncomfortable with the title of this chapter (and this book, for that matter), is correct—that the author, though very human and often a fine example of humankind's propensity for inconsistency, is not a fraud—neither is he as "together" as being a pastor or an author can sometimes imply. While she frets over the possibiity that I may be representing myself as less than I am, my primary fear comes from the possibility that I could give the opposite impression, painting myself in colors that far outshine the reality.

This sensitivity about not presenting yourself as something better than you actually are is one with which I was raised. I suppose that's why I start this book the way I do. I recall a conversation my dad was having with one of his brothers; they were jesting, but their kidding revealed a deep value held by both men.

"My neighbor's kid is a drug dealer, a thief, and an abuser of defenseless animals," said my uncle, "and he's not even shy about it."

My dad responded as though on cue. "Yeah," he said, "but your neighbor should count his blessings. It could have been worse. At least his kid isn't a hypocrite."

The list of sins my father and I discussed as I was growing up varied from petty to potentially deadly. But right up there toward the top of it, definitely in the "potentially deadly" category, was the sin of duplicity. A person could make a variety of mistakes in our family and still feel welcome at the dinner table, but to present yourself as something you weren't, or even to allow yourself to be perceived that way, was definitely not among them.

I suppose that's why I must begin this project by making it very clear that, as I said before, there is sometimes a profound difference between the spirituality for which I long (presented in the following chapters) and the spirituality I live and manifest.

Some years ago I heard a lecture by famed leader Andrew Young, who, as a young pastor, worked for Dr. Martin Luther King Jr. during the Civil Rights Movement. He later became a U.S. Congressman and served for a time as the Mayor of Atlanta, but in his heart he was always a pastor. So I wasn't surprised to hear him quote an old preacher he'd once heard. It was a quote from a message designed to offer hope to a congregation—to help them in their battle against discouragement by reminding them what God had done in the past and could still do for them in the future.

"We ain't what we should be," Young said, quoting that preacher, "and we ain't what we gonna be. But praise God, we ain't what we was!"

As I launch into topics like courage, humility, faith, loyalty, and yieldedness, I must reclaim for myself what that preacher announced. I hunger for the rich spirituality marked by the traits presented in the chapters that follow but have to admit that much of the spirituality I've experience has been marked more by scarcity than richness.

What follows are a few real-life stories that I think serve my point. All of these things happened while I was a pastor. Some of the conversations are from memory and, therefore, not presented verbatim. At a couple of points, I've combined some discussions for the sake of flow and gently embellished others in order to help the reader get a better sense of the mood. Still, everything noted in the stories below was actually communicated, and most of the stories unfolded just as they are presented here, making it painfully clear that the author is, in fact, an authentic, card-carrying hypocrite. Please keep that in mind as you read on.

I love music. In fact, I love it so much it's easy for me to hate some of it—especially when it's poorly presented.

"Grec, people are watching you. They notice that kind of thing." Brenda whispered that to me once while we sat together listening to worship music and waiting to be introduced at a church where I'd been invited to speak. What she was concerned about was the fact that my hands were clenched like vise grips to each side of my chair while I was literally (and visibly) stiffening up and cringing every time a vocalist missed a note or the drummer sped up the cadence.

"I'm trying. Really. But it's painful. What is this, a review of 'The Worst of American Idol'? I mean, we wouldn't have to change a stinkin' thing if we wanted to present this as a *Saturday Night Live* sketch," I whispered through clenched teeth, my mouth having been wrestled into the shape of a completely disingenuous smile.

"It's not that bad. They're doing the best they can. Besides, they're not professionals, and I'm sure there are a thousand places they could be other than here, trying to help us worship. Just listen to the message, not the performance. "

Sometimes my wife's propensity for grace is almost as annoying as her indifference toward pitch and tempo.

"I'm sorry. I can't help it. I just can't stand it when good music is done so poorly—especially when it's *worship* music. And we wonder why kids don't want to attend church services! Maybe what we assign to a waning desire for God on their part is actually the result of them having very good taste in music!" I was still clutching my seat cushion as I leaned away from her ear. I straightened back up in my chair and resurrected my lying grin.

"It's fine, honey." She was unmoved by my pain. "Besides, you'd better deal with it, because you'll be up there in a couple of minutes yourself. They're trying. Just let it go."

"Okay. But there's no way I'm thanking the worship band for the 'great music.' No chance!"

"Whatever."

"I refuse! I'm not doing it!" I protested.

"No one's asking you to. Just try to be kind and remember that not everyone sees it the way you do."

I was about to respond when I realized that the last song had ended and we had to stop talking in order to join in with the congregation's vigorous applause. After being introduced I went to the pulpit and opened my Bible. The first words out of my mouth? You guessed it. "Thanks so much, band, for the worship music. I can't tell you how appreciative I am."

What else *could* I say? First of all, I've already admitted that *the author is a hypocrite;* secondly, I really *did* appreciate ... well ... the fact that it had finally ended.

Who loves going to the dentist? I certainly do not, and I suspect you don't, either. But if there's something I enjoy even less than going to the dentist, it's *paying* to go. That's why I made sure everyone in our family, all three children (then ten, eleven, and twelve) and both of their parents (significantly older) had extensive checkups and received all necessary repairs before the end of the month in August of 1993. Why the rush? Because until the end of that month we had one hundred percent dental coverage. Once the calendar did its normal thing, that was going to change mightily.

So a phone call was made, appointments were scheduled, children were self-organized in protest, and the dentist was visited. Well, he was visited by everyone but me, that is. I was going to have to go a week later, while the rest of my family was away.

I remember kidding each of the children after the reports came back from their checkups. All, of course, would be forced to have their teeth cleaned. "They will keep digging and digging," I taunted, "rubbing your gums in the same place over and over again, until you're ready to scream. They'll poke that sharp, metal needle into the middle of your most sensitive teeth, then deep into your gums, probably making them bleed."

"Stop it! You'll scare them so much they'll never go back. Or maybe *you* want to take them and deal with it next time." This was their mother, defending and assaulting in the same breath.

Unfazed, I went on. "And did anyone have a cavity?"

"All of us did." It was our eldest giving the report. Then, pointing to his younger brother, he added, "Josh had two."

I jumped at my chance. "Oh no!" I said, my face twisted in mock horror. "Do you know what they do when you have a cavity? They take a drill and slowly grind out part of your tooth . . ." Then mimicking the shrill, inconsistent sound of a dentist's drill as it stalled and accelerated, stalled and accelerated, then stalled and accelerated again, I watched as three wide-eyed children grimaced in imagined pain.

They knew I was just kidding. In fact, they had all but demanded some sort of playful ritual every time our family visited the dental torture chamber. Even so, I could see that the predictable "post-dental-checkup torment" still had its desired effect. As though perfectly choreographed, their shoulders hunched. Then, faces already scrunched, each of the three raised a hand in order to cover their mouths.

Mom was not amused. "You're teaching them to hate the dentist, Greg!" This coming from a woman who at that time had never had a cavity and, therefore, never been required to endure the pain of having a tooth drilled.

"That's one way to look at it," I said. "I prefer to think I'm teaching them to always remember to floss."

Brenda just rolled her eyes and left the room. Now that I think of it, she was forced to roll eyes and leave rooms a lot in those days.

When the kids got home from their encounters with the drill a few days later, we all had a great time pronouncing the word "flabbergasted" through fat, comatose, unresponsive lips. No credit did I receive, however, for the genius of using the aftermath of a dentist's needle as an opportunity to make our children giggle and slobber at the same time.

My laughter, however, was short-lived. Because along with the report that the day's appointments had all gone reasonably well came news my family seemed very pleased to give me. It was a report from our dentist about what had been discovered after *my* x-rays and the "slightly uncomfortable procedure" that awaited me only a few days later.

My wife, who had worked for a dentist in the past, lined up our kids so they could enjoy what she was about to say as much as she did. "I'm happy to tell you that when you go to the dentist next week, you'll be needing more than the common cleaning and checkup you were expecting," she reported. "He informed me today that you'll also be having a root canal."

I began to breathe a bit more rapidly.

"Do you know what they do in a root canal?" she asked. Our kids took on the look of anticipation children have just before the cake is brought out at a birthday party. "They almost suffocate you by placing a rubberized sheet over your mouth." Three little smiles were growing wider with each syllable. "Then the dentist not only drills your tooth," all three kids started making the drilling sound I'd taught them—one I'm certain they rehearsed on the way home—"but then takes a little file and painstakingly pulverizes each tiny particle in the middle of your tooth, until he has hollowed out the entire center of each root canal, one . . . delicate . . . nerve . . . at a time."

Now it was my turn to cringe as her thumb and forefinger, miming the pinching of a dentist's file between them, went through the staccato, up-and-down motions of an endodontist with her hand stuffed in a mouth.

"Okay! Enough! Stop!" I begged.

As they ran off, I'm sure I heard Becca, our youngest and our only daughter, holler, "And don't forget to say 'flabbergasted' afterward, Dad."

THREE DAYS LATER

As I entered, I immediately noticed that the dental office had a sort of upscale Costco feel to it. It was a large, square building with twelve-foot ceilings; the entire interior had been divided into several individual cubicles, each of which was defined by eight-foot-high pony-walls. So with four feet between the top of each wall and the ceiling, not one of the examining rooms was as private as it actually felt. The effect was that, though you could see only your dentist and dental assistant, you could hear the sounds of drills and low conversation coming from all directions. What eventually turned out to be even worse for me was the fact that everyone else could also hear you. While I sat in the reception area, waiting for my name to be called, I could feel my heart pounding, like a countdown clock marking the seconds before a bomb went off. Then I heard the two most painful words anyone ever hears in a dental waiting room. They came from a lady wearing a white coat and holding a clipboard. "Art Grayco?" she said just before looking up from her notes.

"My goodness," I said under my breath, "when you're calling a guy to his turn in the torture chamber, could you at least have the decency to pronounce his name right?"

"Gr-*eh*-co," I corrected so all could hear. "Grec . . . as in the word 'heck.'"

Then, under my breath again: "Need me to use that in a sentence? Okay. How 'bout this: what the *heck* is *Grec* doing here?" Fortunately I kept my thoughts to an imperceptible whisper. No sense angering the executioner, or her staff.

"Oh. Sorry. Right this way Mr. Grec—as in heck—o." She smiled. But as I followed her down a long, solemn hallway, I was almost certain I heard her cry out, "Dead man walking!"

When we finally arrived at my "private" exam room in the back of the building, she pointed to a chair that looked a lot like something that belonged on the set of a Dr. Frankenstein movie. "Just sit right here and relax," she teased. "The doctor will be right with you." Then she turned and left.

I sat, and I prayed, but I certainly didn't relax. Having never had a root canal before, I had decided to do some casual research before my appointment by seeking the advice of friends who *had* experienced one. Opinions varied (mostly in regard to the level of awful pain I should expect), but one thing virtually every root canal alumnus recommended was this: "Be sure you ask for nitrous oxide," each one cautioned. "Whatever you do, ask for the gas!" Being someone who had learned well the lesson of taking good advice when offered, I had every intention of doing just that.

"Good morning Mr. 'Greeko'." It was the dental assistant.

"It's Greco. Grec, as in 'heck'. And good morning to you too." Then I decided to get right to the point. "I'm sure I'll need nitrous oxide. Absolutely certain of it. Can you make sure my doctor knows that?" She assured me that she would.

"I'll have to check to see if your insurance requires an extra charge for that, though."

"No problem. I'll pay it no matter what it is. But I'm sure I'll need it . . . you know, just to help with the whole ordeal, I mean procedure."

The explanation of how the gas worked and what it did was simple enough. Some of the instructions given during the actual introduction were almost comical, though. "We're going to strap this cup over your nose, Mr. Grayko." I decided to just give up on the name and concentrate on the nitrous. "Then what I want you to do is just breathe normally. The nitrous will do the rest. It will sort of take the edge off things."

Right, I thought to myself. *You're going to seal off my mouth so I can breathe only through my nose, give me a shot in the cheek with a four-inch-long needle, then shove that same needle directly into my gums. After that you'll grind and drill until the end of my molar is turned to dust and the raw nerves in my tooth have been exposed. Next you'll take a file and slide it up and down inside the nerve canal, repeating that with different-sized files until each of the three nerves is turned to so much useless powder. Attached to my nose is the dispenser of a drug so powerful that, as I inhale it, it will calm me to the point where I'll actually let you do that . . . and then be willing to pay you for the pleasure afterward.*

I listened and heard a child crying on the other side of the wall to my left. The sound of drills swirling and screaming came from just about every direction, and somewhere someone was being told to open their mouth wider, followed by the sound of fluids being sucked unevenly down an assistant's tube. *Trust me, lady,* I went on in my mind. *If this stuff is strong enough to help me tolerate all of that, I'm going to suck in as much of it as you'll dish out.*

"Ma'am," I replied in a now nasal-sounding voice, "no offense, but the last thing I'm thinking about doing right now is breathing normally. However, if I actually start to enjoy this root canal, I'm sure I'll eventually ask you to turn it down."

Thankfully she smiled. Then she ruined the moment by telling me that the doctor would be right with me. As she walked away I closed my eyes, prayed again (mostly for forgiveness), then sucked in the drug-seasoned air as firmly and fully as I could—through my nose, of course.

The procedure seemed to be going well. I could hardly move with the doctor's fingers packed so tightly into my mouth, and I was never quite sure where to look (it seemed that I was always staring him straight in the eyes—too intimate for a root canal), so I just closed my eyes and continued to concentrate on "breathing normally."

Actually, I was a bit surprised by how tolerable it really was. In fact, it started to feel so pleasant I began to think that if it meant using nitrous oxide, it might even be worth it to come back and get another tooth done. That was when a full tray of files, all with different-colored handles, was flashed before my eyes and the next size up was selected. My response? Be more aggressive in my "breathing normally."

"Are you doing okay, Mr. Grayko?"

"Uh-huh." I thought it must have sounded more like a grunt

than anything else. Whether or not he understood it, the doctor seemed to be satisfied with my answer.

But in my head I knew I was inching toward not okay . . . *very, VERY* not okay. In fact, something terrible was happening. I suddenly became convinced of the fact that I was flying and, in fact, dying—right there in the dentist's chair during a common root canal. The special effect was Spielberg-like, giving me the sense that my chair was floating up off of the floor and rushing me toward a huge, shining membrane. My nitrous-bathed brain was convinced that when I punched through that membrane, it would mean I had died and I would be in Heaven. During my ascension a conversation began in my mind. It was an internal argument, really, between my noble mind and my depraved mind. It went something like this:

Noble Mind: You really should tell the doctor that you have inhaled too much nitrous. It's one thing to innocently get too much of it, but you know you're getting too much and it's causing something weird to happen.

Depraved Mind: Don't you dare say a word! If you tell him, he'll turn it down and you won't get to feel all this really cool stuff you're feeling.

Noble Mind: But this is wrong, Art. Plus, you're thinking things about five seconds before they actually occur. So even if you raise your hand right now, it will take five seconds before reality catches up to you and it actually happens. That's five more seconds of gas before the poor doctor even knows anything's wrong. Raise your hand . . . right now!

Depraved Mind: You'll do nothing of the kind. This is perfect! You can get high and technically it isn't even a sin. I mean, you're just getting a sedative at the dentist's office. Besides, the world hasn't felt like it was in such wonderful order since you were a child. Just keep "breathing normally," through your nose, and keep your mouth shut. I mean, isn't that exactly what the assistant told you to do? Besides, this must be what the sixties would have felt like had you been born early enough to experience them as an adult instead of as a grammar school kid. You could apply all of this experiential knowledge to your counseling and preaching. This could actually help you be a more relevant communicator in the long run.

All the while, that membrane was getting closer and closer. Any minute I'd break through to Heaven and meet Jesus. Within seconds I'd see His face, hear the angels, and meet those great saints of the past. I imagined walking around with God as He introduced me to the apostles and some of the big names of the Bible. I was about to be done with taxes, done with dentists, done with life. It was almost time for me to begin my time of unending rest.

That was when my "noble mind" put its foot down and took over completely. I began to think about my wife, my children, a recent argument I had had with my daughter, and of course, my faith. Suddenly that membrane was way too close for comfort. In fact, it seemed as though I was rushing far too quickly toward it now.

And didn't I recall that things hadn't ended so easily for some of those big names I was about to meet? I imagined some of the interviews I was about to have.

"How did you die, sir?"

"I was crucified upside down."

"And you, ma'am?"

"I was sawn in two while my dear children watched and cried out for mercy."

"Oh. Really?"

Then, turning to another in the group I'd inquire, "And you, brother?"

"When I refused to reverse my allegiance to Jesus, I was boiled alive in olive oil. But enough about us," he might say, "how did you come to the end of your life and join our heavenly troop, young man?"

"Who, me?" I would answer as I looked down at my shuffling feet. "Root canal."

I just couldn't let that happen. Die in my sleep? Yes. Hit by a car while crossing the street to get to the library? That would be acceptable. Heart attack while admiring the beauty of Rembrandt's *Prodigal*? I would be proud to tell the story. But "death by root canal" was not going to go over very well behind the pearly gates. I had to at least try to salvage this. Mostly out of vanity and the desire for a halfway honorable "death story," I decided I had to tell the dentist that something was wrong.

I had waited so long, however, that I couldn't afford to take the time for subtlety—especially since, at least as far as my marinated brain perceived it, reality lagged behind decisions by several seconds, as though it was on some sort of broadcast time delay.

So with a rubber tent covering my entire mouth, three different sized files sticking up from one of my rear molars, and a quart of saliva pooling at the entry to my throat, I waved my hands wildly, like the robot in *Lost In Space* when he senses Will Robinson and his family might be in danger, and gurgled out at the top of my lungs, "TOO HIGH! TOO HIGH! TOO HIGH!"

I'm not sure how many times I actually screamed that, but it did the trick. Before I even knew what was happening, I was surrounded by several nurses and staff members. Off came the nitrous tube and on came an oxygen mask. A blood pressure cuff was wrapped around my arm and regular reports were being relayed back and forth. Out came the rubber tent. Away went the files. People were running around as though I was the president and I had just been shot. It was crazy.

The dentist, whom I discovered later was fresh out of dental school and in his first week of work, looked down at me with a worried expression and tried to offer comfort. With the quivering voice of a seventh grader asking his favorite girl if she wanted to dance, he said, "Everything is going to be okay, Mr. Grayko. You'll be fine . . . just breathe normally."

I didn't have the heart to just die there and ruin his young career without encouraging him somehow. So I decided to bless him—offer him some comfort. After all, isn't that what good pastors do? Looking up at him there in our "private" examination room, I said, through sloppy lips and with the assistance of a thick, uncooperative tongue and a body still fully under the influence,

"No. I'm going to die today. But I don't want you to quit. You keep being a good dentist. I forgive you for this. Don't quit. Do you hear me?"

He was the struggling Notre Dame football team and I was Knute Rockne in the locker room at halftime.

Then, with the unacceptable thought of only being able to answer "root canal" when the great saints I was about to meet asked me how my life had come to such an early end, I decided to go out with a bang. First I would give some last instructions to my dentist (a man I had met for the first time that day) to deliver to my family.

"Tell my wife that I love her and that I kept my marriage vow. I was faithful. And tell my daughter that she and I are good—that I thought she was *fantastic* and that I'm sorry that I communicated so poorly with her."

But that wasn't all I had in mind. At the peak of the entire event I decided that I should not go passively. No. I should tell people about Jesus and my feelings for him. So, as loudly as I could possibly shout, I began to cry out, "I LOVE JESUS! I LOVE JESUS! I LOVE JESUS!"

This was the true me. I was committed! Under the unshackling influence of an overdose of nitrous oxide, I was not ashamed to be a Christian. I was Joan of Arc being burned alive without recanting; I was William Wallace demanding freedom while being skinned alive and not backing down. I was going to be able to say to the greatest names in Heaven that I had expired while spilling my guts for Christ and announcing to everyone that he was the one who came to save the world.

I don't know exactly how long it took for me to quit screaming out the Lord's name, but I do remember the shock of realizing that the membrane through which I was going to burst as I entered Heaven was actually nothing more than the large, round light every dentist has hanging over their patient chairs. And how can I find the words to describe the level of sudden, fraud-revealing fear I felt when I realized that my chair was actually quite securely fixed to the floor, a floor that was in a cubical, a cubical next to another cubical, in a very large room full of cubicles—a now very *hushed* room full of cubicals? By the time that happened, there was only one assistant with me. She was wrapping things up, like that last firefighter coiling hoses after an inner-city blaze, and placing something she had written into my file. Fully in my right mind now and breathing quite normally, I broke the silence.

"I think I sort of dreamed some things," I started. She just kept working in silence. "Did I maybe get a little crazy and perhaps a bit loud?"

"You could say that, yes." She was trying to hold back a smile now. I could tell.

"Well, do you recall what I might have said? 'Cause I'm not sure if it happened or if I just dreamt it all."

Please say I dreamt it all. PLEASE, I silently pleaded. After all, it was fine for me to believe I was someone who could or should be publically unashamed of his faith, but quite *another* thing to actually act that out.

"Sure. You yelled out that you loved God and you loved your wife. That was pretty much it."

"Oh no. That's what I was afraid of. I'm so sorry. And where is that young doctor? I want to apologize to him too," I said, trying to get up out of my chair.

"Oh. He had to cancel the rest of his appointments and just go home for the rest of the day. He was pretty shaken up by the whole episode." There was a short silence before she stopped what she was doing and looked right at me. "May I ask you a question?"

I didn't really want her to, but I nodded anyway.

"You don't need to be sorry for anything you said while you were getting too much nitrous. And you *were* getting too much. You didn't hear this from me, but the machine malfunctioned and you were getting no oxygen in that mix for a little bit there—straight nitrous gas. Anyway, why would anything you said in those few minutes be something you had to apologize for? Please tell me you really believe what you said. I really need to hear that right now."

I responded with full pastoral confidence. But it was the kind of confidence that comes only when one knows he'll be able to leave everything and everyone behind, never again to be seen. As long as that cubical was Vegas, and everything that happened in Vegas stayed in Vegas, I was fine with standing by what I had done.

"Oh yes. Completely. No question. There's no need to apologize or be ashamed of anything I said. Not embarrassed at all. Not in the least bit." But I could tell she was a little let down by my backpedaling.

"Good. We're all done for today then, Mr. Grayko. You'll have to make another appointment for tomorrow so we can finish up," she said without looking up from her work.

I was happy to leave until I realized that everyone in the building would have heard all that went on. "Tell me, is there another way out of here? I'm parked in the back of the building and I can't see any reason for walking all the way back up front and through that lobby full of people." It was a straight-up lie. Truth was, I didn't want to risk being identified as the "I Love Jesus guy" by all those shocked patients in the waiting room.

"Sorry," she answered, "there's only one way in and out. Besides, you'll need to make that appointment for tomorrow morning so we can finish."

I was heartsick. I certainly didn't want to be recognized after being responsible for such drama. But as I walked to the front, I saw that several people, a couple of them older men, were also coming out to pay their bills or make follow-up appointments. No one would have to know I was the one who had played the part of the street-corner preacher in the dentist's office. I'd step up, make my appointment, and quietly leave, anonymity intact. I believed all I had confessed, but I was also happy to find a way to conceal it. After all, remember, the author is a hypocrite.

"I need a follow-up, please. Tomorrow morning if possible."

It was working. After suggesting a time, one I agreed to almost before the receptionist was finished offering it, I turned to leave. I was only three steps from the door when, just as I was reaching for the handle, a big voice, one that everyone in that crowded waiting room turned to listen to, called to me from behind. It was one of the nurses—the one who had been taking and reporting my blood pressure as I returned to reality from the virtual gates of Heaven.

"Well, well, well," she almost shouted, way too playfully for my liking, "no more nitrous oxide for *you*, Mr. Greeko."

In the seemingly synchronized, slow-motion movement of a crowd watching a tennis ball fly from one side of the net to the other, everyone in that waiting room turned their gaze from her to me. I just stared straight ahead, opened the door, and left, very frustrated that there was no back exit in that place.

My duplicity had been uncovered by a rookie dentist, a malfunctioning nitrous oxide machine, and an exaggerated need to appear to be "appropriate" in public. Very bold about the unguarded statements of love for Christ that I had made while legally intoxicated, once I had regained my "sobriety" I was ashamed of having ever made them at all.

You see? The author is a hypocrite.

My spiritual director is a very insightful person. That's a good trait for a spiritual director to have, so I'm glad it's true of mine. He and I have been meeting for direction for several years, each meeting serving like gold deposits into my relatively empty spiritual vault. Especially rich has been his central theme of not only seeing God in everything but seeing everything through God. One of our goals was to develop in me a more mature ability to yield to Him—especially in circumstances over which I had little or no control.

"Never deal with anyone directly," my Episcopal friend with Eastern Orthodox leanings and a huge stable of Evangelical, Protestant friends would say. "In fact, never see or deal with *anything* directly. Always deal with people and see everything that comes into your life through Jesus. Never directly. Always indirectly."

This concept was so compelling that I decided to make it a central focus in my spiritual trek. I was going to learn it, practice it, preach it, and even counsel it. I was determined to see Jesus in everything and everything through Jesus—not that God *is* everything, but that He is *capable* in everything, that He uses everything, that He is always ready to show Himself, regardless of what happens or who comes across my path.

I couldn't wait to start sharing this insight, like an adolescent boy who wants to drive his new car whether or not he really has anywhere in particular to go. Suddenly it was as though every challenge anyone in my church had was the result of an inability to see people and/or circumstances indirectly.

My commitment to this concept was seriously tested one year during an anniversary cruise with my favorite lady. We had been married for thirty-three years, and we were going to celebrate it with one of our favorite things to do together: a cruise.

We realized relatively early in our vacationing career that cruises could be a tremendous value. Mention the word "cruise" to some people and their minds go straight to thoughts of opulence, excess, greed, and hedonism. For us, cruises mean value (if you were going to take a nice, fun vacation anyway) and lots of time together meeting people and making new friends. For about half the cost of renting a condo and spending a week together at Disneyland, we could sail to some of the best beaches in the world, eat wonderful food, go on really fun dates every evening, read book after book, and never have to lift a finger to cook or clean. Brenda and I are always excited to be able to go on a cruise together, and this one was to be no different.

After packing the day before, we got up at four a.m. on the day our ship was to sail and drove from our home just north of San Francisco to Los Angeles with plenty of time to board and get moved into our room. Next was the excitement of exploring our floating home and learning our way around, followed by the mandatory trip up the stairs to the top deck to watch as we slowly sailed out of San Pedro harbor and out to sea. It was a great day and we were in for a wonderful time together. We felt like two little kids on the last day of school. All was going just as we'd hoped.

One of our favorite parts of a cruise is sitting down to dinner with a group of people we've never met, and we were certainly rewarded for that preference on this trip. The other three couples were a perfect fit for us, and we looked forward to seeing them again the next evening. John and Dee were in their mid-eighties and had been married for over sixty years. History was his love, spunkiness was hers. Though they'd been around the block a few times, they were as spry and full of life as anyone in the dining room—and they were both Italian. John, in fact, had even been born in Italy. Wonderful.

Jeff and Andrea were natural emcees, laughing easily and drawing out the funniest sides of the rest of us. They had been married for about twenty-five years and it was pretty obvious that every one of those years had been good to them. She was an artist and he a salesman. They lived in the desert, and Brenda and I were sure they were an oasis to everyone who lived there with them.

John and Tammy were a young couple who had been married for five years. They were from Canada, and seemed to be exceedingly pleased to be anywhere but home in mid-January. John had been on twenty-five cruises and was already planning the next one. That meant, we joked around the table, that he had started cruising somewhere around the age of five and been on one every year of his life since.

Ours was the loud table—the comics' table—the "joy" table. So well matched were we that after about one hour together we had known each other for twenty years. When dinner was over (we were the last ones still seated in the enormous dining room), we were sad to leave and couldn't wait until we got to sit together again. We left with the assignment to bring pictures the next evening and to come ready to talk about the events of the day.

But the next night, the day before our anniversary, there was an empty seat at our "table for eight." Brenda attended dinner without me. When the others asked where I was, she had to explain that I had been detained, "placed under house arrest," as I told it, for a minimum of forty-eight hours in our room. Only then, I was told, would there be a possibility of parole, restoring to me the privilege of wandering the ship once again. She told them that I would not be joining them for our evening meal that day and, though there was some hope of the restrictions being lifted soon, no one would give me a guarantee of when that might happen.

Confined to my cabin, I had been told in no uncertain terms and in the strictest language possible that if I so much as stepped through my cabin door to stretch my legs, I would be more forcefully and dramatically confined, then put off the ship at the next port. Furthermore, if that happened, there would be no reimbursement for cruise days lost, and no assistance whatsoever with me getting back to Los Angeles.

Apparently there were some crimes committed aboard a cruise ship that just couldn't be forgiven, and I had committed one of them. I had committed the crime of diarrhea. The sentence? An unwanted but apparently mandatory medical exam for which I was forced to pay and a minimum of forty-eight hours in solitary confinement. I was being sent to "the hole" and forced to pay a physician for the privilege of going. Some anniversary trip!

I had a bucket of questions, none of which were asked with any degree of grace or understanding. I asked about reimbursement for the cruise days I missed and the exam I was required to have. I asked about fairness. I asked about the possibility that this was an elaborate joke where I was being "punked" (I quickly checked the examining room for hidden cameras and looked to see if Ashton Kutcher was hiding around the corner with a bunch of my giggling Marin County pastor friends in tow). As a last resort, I even asked the properly British nurse/judge that had delivered the sentence at my arraignment how much it was worth to her to simply forget I had ever gone downstairs to try to buy the package of Imodium that had landed me in the doctor's office in the first place.

"Just close your eyes and count slowly to twenty," I offered. "When you open them again, you'll find $60 in cash sitting where I'm sitting now. Would that work for you as well as it would work for me?" I asked. She didn't bite.

But there were some questions you can be sure I never asked. I never asked myself, "Where do you see God showing Himself in this challenge, Art? How do you think He might want to use this situation to shape your heart or direct your life? What would it look like to deal with this nurse and the prison sentence she is required by law to deliver to you INDIRECTLY, THROUGH JESUS?"

I had plenty of questions for everyone else, though. In fact, instead of seeking a way for the unexpected solitude (and awful food) to become my teacher, I began the discipline of regular, nagging phone calls to the medical staff. When I wasn't calling them, begging for an early release, I was asking Brenda (a nurse herself) to go down and see what she could do. Still being detained on the day of our anniversary was the last straw.

"Tell them I took the medicine she gave me and everything is fine now," I begged my wife. "Inform them that I went 'big boy potty,'" (yes, my cynicism was so well honed that I actually did use the term "big boy potty") "and that I'm more than ready to be released. You're a nurse. Use your nursing clout. Just go and talk some of your 'nursing talk.' They'll believe you."

"Honey." Brenda was sympathetic but knew that the ship's medical staff was right. "They have to do this. You wouldn't want them to sit back and just do nothing to protect passengers if you were feeling well and there was the risk of something spreading through the ship, would you? You'd be the first to demand they keep a sick passenger confined to his room—if you weren't that sick passenger."

"Yeah. But I'm not sick. This is something else. I feel great. And trust me, being in lockdown tonight isn't quite what I had in mind. Instead of wearing a tux and eating a nice steak for our anniversary, we're sitting here in our cabin dining on frozen vegetables and clear broth. Tell her that if he doesn't get out of here soon, your husband is going to eat his way through the wall and all the way to the dining room!" She rolled her eyes, then went to talk with the doctors. Secretly, I was sure it was an errand of hopelessness.

Fifty hours and two intolerable dinners later (meals, by the way, that actually *did* put my stomach at risk), I was released into the custody of my good wife, with strict instructions to stay away from the buffet for at least two more days. That night Brenda and I returned to our dinner table to the applause of the other three couples. We all laughed freely as I told the story of my last two days. But inwardly I was still stewing, running through the mental list of attorneys I might ask to lead the charge in my suit against the cruise line for unlawful detainment.

Here's the rub: eight or ten weeks before we left for that vacation, I had been preaching a Sunday series that led me to a message about often-used "church sayings" that were actually not true. In that message, I had explained that one of the least helpful of all was the assertion that "God has a purpose for everything."

"That's actually not true," I challenged. "If that statement is true, it can imply some pretty mean-spirited things about God. What *is* true is that 'God has everything for His purpose.' In other words, whether the stuff of our lives is the result of divine intent and activity or the natural consequences of our own decisions, God can and will use it for His purpose, His agenda on earth. So," I suggested to my church, "perhaps we would all do well to stop asking why this or that happened to us and start asking how we might see God in it, and/or be redirected by Him *through* it."

It wasn't more than a couple of months after I preached that sermon that we boarded our cruise ship and I started the jail-time whining that revealed to me just how easy it was for a man to choke on his own words. Apparently I was much more eager and able to preach things than I was to actually live them. I was keen to "see God in everything," except the things that actually happened to me.

See? I *warned* you. The author is a hypocrite!

We had been at our new call as pastor and wife for only a few months—fifteen weeks, to be more precise—when our first Christmas there landed on us.

Brenda and I were in what easily made the "top-two list" of the handful of painfully impassioned arguments of our then twenty-seven years of marriage. Though always fun to reconcile, those fights were never much fun to experience. And in the case of *this* battle, both the execution and the reconciliation were bound to take a while.

What made it even worse was that, at a crucial crescendo in the engagement, we were already late for one of the most celebrated events of our new church's year: the Borsari family Christmas Eve party. Some of the most influential people in our new church would be there, the wine would be flowing (and trust me, none of it would come from spouted boxes purchased at a local grocery store), and most eyes would be on the new pastor and his wife. Not a good setting for a freshly angered Italian clergyman and his equally charged redheaded Irish wife to make an early impression, especially on an already deeply fractured but potentially great church.

We were parked outside the party when that crescendo hit.

This particular argument had started months earlier, really— before we had moved back to California to give pastoral leadership to our new congregation. I had been very, very, VERY happy to no longer be the leader of a local church. In fact, during my earliest years as a pastor, I had felt so ill-fitted that I used to argue with God on occasion, contending that he had called me to a life for which he had forgotten to equip me.

I have an incredible lack of patience, and a complete inability to differentiate a parishioner's tragedy from my own daily emotions and life rhythms. For instance, the idea that I could dare go home and joyfully play with our young children if only recently one of our church's members had watched me bury one of hers was unthinkable. I mean, how could I do something like that if I really cared about those I served?

But wait. There's more. I possess a seemingly cosmic propensity for arrogance, looking down my nose at anyone who: has two first names as a first name (i.e. Billy-Bob or Linda-Lou); a tendency to use double negatives and speak too loudly in public settings; or a willingness to boldly display the number of his/ her favorite Nascar driver in the rear window of a pickup truck. As for tempers, mine can be an explosive one that, in its most destructive phases, lapses into cynicism quicker than a hungry frog laps up a meandering fly. Add all of this to things far too personal or embarrassing to note here, and the insanity of God placing me in a position that is designed to lead dear people into lives of unity, compassion, and mercy becomes destructively obvious.

There was another problem: In addition to being emotionally unsuited for it, I hadn't really *wanted* to be at this party. In fact, I never *wanted* to move or become the pastor of that church. My preference would have been to stay with the denominational job I had left to come west.

So why, you might ask, had I left that denominational position and accepted the call back to a local pastorate in the first place? To answer that question, we have to go back to the last church I had pastored and a phone call I received five and a half years into my surprisingly enjoyable tenure there.

December, 2003: Arvada, Colorado

"Art?" It was my secretary on the intercom. "You have a call on line one. Should I put it through?"

"Depends," I answered. "Who is it? I'm swamped. And I'm way behind on this week's sermon."

On the line was a good friend with a question that shocked me. Would I ever consider taking a position with our denomination, the Evangelical Covenant Church? It would mean a move from Denver to Chicago, but it was to be a sort of "traveling/

teaching/encouraging/strategizing" ministry to the hundreds of churches we had in the U.S. and Canada.

At that point, I had never even *thought* of such a thing, much less considered it. I'd finally found peace as a local minister there in Denver and, for the first time I could remember, was even enjoying it. Coming to work every day was downright fun, and the team there was comprised of close and thoroughly compatible friends. Most important of all, our church was getting healthier every year.

There were other reasons to stay put, too. Brenda's sister and her husband had just moved to the area to take over leadership of the *Denver Post.* We finally lived near family again. Plus, Denver and I have things in common—one of them being a love for sports. Our church was loaded with Broncos season ticketholders, most of whom loved to take me to games, and one of my best friends was the television broadcaster for the Colorado Rockies, so I occasionally got to watch games from the broadcast booth. Who leaves a situation like that?

Still, the thought of a career change was intoxicating. I had made the cardiologically fatal mistake of actually falling in love with that Denver congregation, and they had certainly been good to me. But after significant discussion and the encouragement of the two family members who would have been most affected by a move, I decided that the challenge of the unknown just wouldn't let go of me. I decided to make the change, and called to tell my friend I was interested in his offer. Eight weeks later I was starting a new life, in a new city, with an entirely new set of standards, rhythms, and measures. I had come from a positive church experience to my new denominational charge. Even so, during the five years I was in that new job, I discovered that there was a lot about not pastoring a church (even one I loved so much) that I liked. I grew fond of weeks that didn't include the regular but often unrecognized pressure of a looming sermon, days off that were really days off, and being fully there after coming home in the evening. For the first time in decades, major holidays could be enjoyed unencumbered by the pastoral responsibilities that usually attended them. My salary was better; my heart was definitely lighter; and laughter was not only deeper, but much more easily found. I lost weight that was actually staying off, and sleep seemed to come quickly, peacefully, and deeply.

Even more satisfying was the fact that I felt as though I was making a potentially relevant contribution to the things that mattered most to me—maybe even a more strategic one than at any other time in my life.

Not being a pastor had led to a place of pleasure about which I had forgotten. In spite of the fact that my new position forced us to live where it was necessary to own a snowblower and a heavy winter coat, I liked our new life very much.

Then, nearly eleven months *before* we sat in our car outside the Borsari home in California, this argument—it was a prolonged mini-war, really—was launched. The battle started as so many disagreements do: innocently.

February, 2004: Our home in Rolling Meadows, Illinois

"Guess what happened to me today at the meetings," I said to my spouse one evening. "I was approached by one of our leaders and asked if I would be interested in returning to California as a pastor. She even mentioned the names of a couple specific churches."

"Were any of them close to home? Close to our families?"

"Yeah," I said, not quite picking up on her interest, "two were within five hours' drive, but they are both pretty established—nothing really broken and in need of obvious repair. I don't want to drive a car someone else has already fully restored. The other one was actually only about ninety minutes' drive from your mom's place. Crazy, huh?"

Her response surprised me. "And you said?"

"I said no, of course. It would mean being a pastor again. I'd have to be insane to leave this position to go back to that. When was the last time you saw one of our denominational administrators who used to be a pastor leave his or her position to go back to that craziness? Almost never. And there's a reason for that: It's because our administrators aren't masochists!"

"Some have gone back," she countered, "and I *know* you aren't meaning to imply that only a self-destructive person would choose to be a pastor."

"Yeah. Pretty much," I replied, always the master cynic.

Her silent tears—tears she was obviously trying to hide as she asked if I had eaten, then calmly left the room—told me that this was the *beginning* of a discussion, not the end. I was right. Over the next several months we had an on-and-off dance with the idea of leaving a world and lifestyle I had come to enjoy and returning to one I was happy to have left behind. It was a conversation that bounced from how wonderful it would be to be able to drive forty minutes to meet one of her sisters or her mom for lunch on a moment's notice to how awful it would be for me to risk re-entering the torturous yet familiar battle with depression that might result from being a local church pastor again.

"Besides," I pointed out, "how often does a pastor get to lead a church and a staff as fantastic as the one we left behind in Denver? Not very often. If I were going to continue as a pastor, I'd have never left *them*. No way!"

Later in our decision process, we sought input from close advisors, most of whom affirmed my reluctance, reminding us that the church we were considering in California was rumored to be quite unhealthy. It was so broken, in fact, that some of our closest friends even called to implore us not to go—or at least to go somewhere else, *anywhere* else.

"That church is a black hole of clergy destruction" was the message being communicated by one friend. "I don't want to see you get sucked into it and devoured."

Making things even tougher was the fact that the intricacies affecting what we did were multiplied virtually every day. The most troubling of those had to do with some of the people closest to us.

We had recently received a phone call informing us that my mother-in-law had been found draped over the steering wheel of her hastily parked car. Unconscious, she had been rushed to the hospital—a hospital three thousand miles, two time zones, and a three or four-day drive from us. My mother (whom Brenda loved almost as strongly as she loved hers) was declining rapidly while contending faithfully and courageously, if not effectively, with a debilitating disease of her own. Surely, I wondered, it couldn't be that choosing my own health (if remaining in Chicago was what that required) should cost our own moms *theirs.* And what kind of sibling would be willing to leave all the responsibilities of caring for ailing parents in the hands of their sisters and brothers—especially when three of them were being kicked around by physical and financial challenges of their own?

The decision was a no-win. Stay in Chicago, and I could avoid the noose of parish ministry, but at the cost of my wife's joy and maybe even our parents' health. Go back to California, and we could be near our families again and back in our home state after being gone for nearly twenty-five years, but I wasn't at all sure I could survive the stress of another tenure in a church.

"Great!" I would complain. "No matter what we decide, at least one of us has to lose."

Ours certainly never approached the complexity or severity of decisions other people make every day. We understood that. But it was a challenging and difficult process nonetheless.

Eventually, though, we began to get some clarity. It came without the calm and assurances one hopes for, but at least it came. I hated it, resisted it, despised it, even tried to out-reason it. What I never figured out, however, was how to avoid it. Once I admitted that this was a decision to be made not on the basis of ease but duty, I found myself trapped in a corner of awful, painful, foul-tasting clarity. I had only one option, and I didn't like it at all.

She never said it, but I knew it would have been unfair for me to continue to ask my wife to live so far away from our increasingly needy parents. The nurse in her would be tortured daily if we stayed. When I suggested I was concerned for her and I thought we needed to go back home, Brenda's response made it clear my suspicions were dead on.

"We can't make this decision based on me being so far from my family," she said. "I'm coping much better, and I'm pretty sure I'll be fine."

"Coping much better" wasn't anything I recalled promising to help my bride do on the day we took our marriage vows. I mean, as much as I tried, I just couldn't remember saying anything like, ". . . and I promise to love, cherish, and respect you, helping you to 'cope much better' when my career causes you to deny the deepest longings of your ever-growing heart."

My vocational vows had come face to face and into direct conflict with my marriage vows. And it was time for me to finally allow the marital vows to take precedence. So with no sense of peace, no compliance from my own heart, and candidly, no true desire to do so, I called and accepted the California position that had been offered to me.

That, looking back on it, was when this pre-Christmas party argument that would come to a head eleven months later had *really* started. It was as though I had planted a garden without pulling the weeds. For growing alongside my desire to care for my wife was an ever-present disgust with the realization that the means of doing so was a return to the pastorate. I was convinced of two conflicting things at the same time: 1) that this was what I had to do; and 2) that the price tag for being a good husband was the abandonment of any hope of ever being truly happy—at least until my blessed and much-anticipated day of retirement.

"Oh joy," I thought to myself, "only seventeen years of faithful misery until I can smile again. But hey, look on the bright side. At least my wife can have an occasional hamburger and shopping spree with her mom and sisters." It was pretty clear that I had made the right choice, but with the wrong heart. I was cynically obedient, faithfully miserable, and that made me no fun to be around.

That was still my prevailing attitude when we pulled up late to our new friends' party that night. And I was unobstructed in my ability to express it.

Back to December, 2004, the day we were parked outside the Christmas party in California

It had been more than six months since I had formally agreed to accept this new pastorate, and a little over three months since my arrival. Still, little had changed in my heart. In fact, my level of frustration had actually increased since we made the move. Even though I truly adore her, I temporarily resented my mother-in-law for getting sick (she had since discovered that her struggles were the result of a pharmacy's mistake and had no direct connection to any serious illness); I resented the fact that my wife couldn't find a way to quit missing me in the role of pastor (even though her heart for the local church and love for people has always been one of my greatest assets); and I resented God for the terrible trick He had played on me (even though I often thank Him for doing it now).

It seemed as though my veins had been filled with bitter juice, and it was my Christian duty to either stuff all of my truest feelings into the sleeves of my Bible and attend the festive party that had started on time and was therefore already in full swing, or drive away with at least some table scrap of integrity left. It was decision time, as we sat there stewing in our car.

"Are we going in?" Brenda asked, breaking the pseudo-calm of an internally noisy silence.

My response was rude. But it was a *Christian* rudeness, the kind that justifies itself by hiding behind the mask of truth— as though the fact that something is honestly felt or at least partially accurate automatically means it should be spoken.

"You know, we wouldn't be in this stinking mess if you could just get your arms around the fact that you're supposed to leave your mother and cleave to your husband! Half of the people in that house," I moaned, pointing to the front door, "are willing to give me a chance, and the other half will celebrate with another party the day I fail here. In fact, that woman with the really curly hair, the one that sent us the box of Brie . . . what's her name?"

"Percie Samialson. You really do need to work on those names."

"Yeah, her. And who, by the way, names their daughter 'Percie'? The other night at prayer meeting, she actually suggested that I have a demon and that I was going to be the ruin of this church. She said God had told her that I was loved by Him and meant well, but that I was possessed. Can you believe that? She's here tonight—somewhere behind that door over there—and she'll expect me to smile and hug her as though we graduated high school together and have been friends ever since. This church is going to be my undoing! And now we have to go in and find a way to pretend to be happy we're here? And as if that weren't bad enough, I'll then have to go and preach a wonderful, joyful, lighthearted Christmas Eve message at multiple services right afterward." I was really heated and loud now. "I love you, but I'm really struggling with you right now," I conceded.

Brenda was calm and logical. "Look. You act as though everyone is against you. What about the Borsaris? You really like them. And you know *they're* glad we're here. Alan's here, too. Both of those guys let you live in their homes while I was in Chicago waiting for the house to close. Just hang with *them*."

My wife was right. Everything she said made sense. But I wasn't listening. The self-absorption of inner rage was winning the day, and I couldn't see that changing for some time.

"We don't have to go in." It was the passenger seat talking again. "We can drive off and talk this out—maybe even pray together—or we can go in and fake our way through the evening. But we can't just sit out here in front of the house and do nothing. What do you want to do, Grec?" Brenda asked.

I thought for a moment, then turned off the engine, opened my door, looked to her and said, "Put on your happy face. We're going in. If God is determined to sentence me to this, I might as well try to make the best of it."

We locked the car, walked to the front door, straightened our clothes, and rang the bell.

Our host seemed happy enough to see us. "Hey, everyone! Look who's here! It's our new pastor and his wife. Welcome, welcome, Grecos."

"Really glad we could come," I lied. "Thanks so much for inviting us. Merry Christmas!"

If we'd had text bubbles over our heads as we walked through the door, mine would have read something like, "Angry, unresolved, not smiling inside, and definitely not in the Christmas spirit; doesn't expect to be for some time to come and wishes you had never asked him to take this job." Hers would have simply presented the words: "I'm doing the best I can to be warm and gracious, but he broke my heart while we were arguing out in the car just now. Please go easy on me."

Glad for the emotional anonymity a good party can often protect, we entered to hugs, grins, and the first of many glasses of Pinot, Cab, and Merlot. I, of course, was just fine, gladhanding and joking. No problem at all for such a well-practiced actor.

Folks, if there's one thing I can say with certainty, it's this: I am the owner of a powerful ability to believe and assert one thing but do something that is entirely other. Let there be no question about it: THE AUTHOR IS AN OSCAR-WINNING HYPOCRITE. If you are still comfortable reading what he has to say about something as important and central to life as spirituality after knowing that, then go ahead and turn the page or push the button to confront these seven marks of a truly healthy spirituality. But if you do that, I suggest you also remember to employ the advice I heard from a camp speaker the first time I went on a religious retreat back in 1975. "Be sure to eat the meat but spit out the bones," he cautioned. To that I offer a huge, embarrassing, California "Ditto!"

A prayer for potential hypocrites:

"Oh Lord who sees things as they actually are and in light of how they actually should be, hunt down the duplicity in me—even the propensity for duplicity—and defeat it, I pray. Take it by the ankles and fling it into the deepest, darkest waters available to you. And in so doing, grant me the freedom that comes with its demise. Amen."

CHAPTER TWO
HUMILITY

Humility is "the framework within which all virtue lives."

HUMILITY:

The Willingness to Be Perceived as Insignificant in Order to Be Effective

My friend Ron and I have a lot in common. He's a pastor just east of Sacramento, California. I pastor a church a couple of hours west of him. He's a football coach at a local high school. I coached high school football for several years as well. He started a church early in his career. I started a church early in my career. He wore a kilt to his church one Sunday morning. I . . . okay, our lives aren't a perfect parallel. But we've become fun and close friends over the years. For obvious reasons, our friendship has developed pretty naturally, and we are always looking for the next opportunity to hang out together.

One year when I was living in Chicago, Ron called with an idea I couldn't resist. "Hey, Grec, what if you came out here to warm, sunny California and did a seminar at out church? You could come out early, visit your folks, then come up on Friday night and hang with me on the sidelines during our biggest game of the season."

I considered it a brilliant idea and bought my ticket the minute I hung up the phone.

Ron is an excellent pastor. But he's also a very, very good high school football coach. Dressed in his team's colors, I stood behind his kneeling team as Ron gave a rousing talk about

how important it was that they pay attention and play well—
especially that night, against their rivals. I was impressed
but not surprised by the way Ron handled his players during
warm-ups, too—arm around one as he offered encouragement,
banging the pads of another while shouting wild predictions
of how unfortunate it was going to be for any player that was
forced to line up across from him during the evening's contest.

At game time I took my place on the sideline, excited to have
the opportunity to watch Ron call offensive plays and, of course,
to offer advice about which plays he should consider running—
advice he wisely ignored. As the game progressed, though,
I began to notice something. There was a telling difference
between the players on the field and those who were on the
sidelines with me. It was kind of funny, and I chuckled at the
fact that I could have been coaching for so many years and
never noticed it with any of my own teams, especially since I
was sure it had been true with them too. It had to do with the
way players looked, the way they dressed in their uniforms.

The players on the field, the ones with the soiled uniforms,
obviously spent most of their time concentrating on their
football abilities and the challenges they might face in the game.
Almost to the man, they wore pretty basic and always filthy
shoes, had helmets with dents, scars, and no shortage of dirt on
them, and seemed unconcerned with the fact that their socks,
which in some cases didn't even match, hung loosely around
their ankles. There was little that could be considered "fancy"
about most of these guys, at least not when it came to the way
they suited up for the game.

When it came to playing football, these young men were
obviously too busy focusing on *being* football players to worry

that much about *looking* like football players. There was almost a strange sort of humility about them. If looking insignificant in pregame drills was what it took for them to be effective on the field of play, they were willing to look insignificant. For the men on the field, it was more important to *be* good than to look good.

In contrast I noticed that many of the kids standing with me on the sideline, the ones who rarely entered the actual game, looked spectacular. They came with embroidered towels hanging from their belts, gloves that matched the color of their towels, shiny, clean helmets, manicured black strips placed perfectly under their eyes, and tape so thoughtfully laced around their shoes and ankles that from a distance they appeared to be wearing spats. These guys were color-coded, with perfectly placed wristbands, designer elbow pads, and uniforms cleaned and pressed.

But they never played. Unlike the sloppy-looking champions who actually ran the ball and made the tackles, these members of my friend's team almost seemed to care more about *looking* good than actually *being* good. Looking like players was much more important to them than actually being players, and I imagined that the thought of taking less time with their outfits in order to take more time with their playbooks was something that never crossed their minds.

Sadly, what I saw on that fall evening is a pretty good illustration of the way some of us approach spirituality. Like those "bench players" on Ron's team, sometimes we find that we're more interested in the adornments of spirituality than in the actual practice of it—that we would rather *look* good than *be* good. And that's a problem, because the socks of true spirituality rarely match or fit right, the uniforms are almost

never clean, and the shoes are usually caked in so much dirt
and field muck that the issue of how well or how often they're
shined is irrelevant.

Jerry Maguire was right: Life's "an up-at-dawn, pride-
swallowing siege."[2] That's also uniquely true for the spiritual
journey. There's always a strange and lingering humility in true
spirituality, and it never looks quite as tidy and ordered in the
real game as it does in the team picture. But you can't find the
real thing without it. The pathway to substantial spirituality is
always substantial humility. Perhaps that's why so many of us
settle for making the squad, wearing the uniform, and posing
for the picture, but are relatively slow to develop any real drive
to leave the sidelines.

Truth? If going deep spiritually means going deep in humility,
too many of us would rather look spiritually deep than actually
be spiritually deep.

The title of this chapter comes from a lecture I heard by one of
my favorite teachers, Dr. David Nystrom. I loved the way he
put it but remember feeling temporarily uncomfortable with
the phrase, too. Later I uncovered the source of my discomfort.
It was the realization that many people in Christian churches
around our country would be secretly offended by his words.
I say "secretly" because disagreement would rarely be publicly
admitted. The way we actually live, pray, and think, though,
seems to be more aligned with a t-shirt slogan I once saw:
"GALILEO WAS WRONG. THE UNIVERSE *DOES*

REVOLVE AROUND ME!" than with the assertion Nystrom made in his excellent talk.

This chapter is about the difference between Dr. Nystrom's proposition and the sentiment on that t-shirt. It's intended to be a challenge to quit talking like we agree with the professor but living as though we believe the t-shirt. It's an invitation to grow in humility and an introduction to a definition of humility that might actually help that growth happen.

Some of the greatest names in Christian history have gone out of their way to make it clear that, though all of the classic virtues are important, humility is the most important of all. Augustine said of it that it was the first, second, and third precepts of the Christian faith.[3] Wesley called it "the center of all virtues."[4] It figures prominently in the Rule of St. Benedict, put forth as one of the few qualities through which a man or woman is distinguished in God's sight.[5] Thomas A. Kempis submits that it's the foundation of true greatness.[6] But Bernard of Clairvaux may have said it best when he wrote, "Humility is the true and solid foundation of all virtues. For if humility were to collapse, the building-up of the virtues will fall down."[7]

The importance of humility has not been lost on contemporary thinkers, either. Henry Nouwen spoke of it as "the real Christian virtue. . . . It is the virtue that opens our eyes for the presence of God on the earth and allows us to live grateful lives."[8] It's been argued that we "experience humility not because we have fought and lost but because humility is the only lens through which great things can be seen,"[9] and it's even been assigned the lofty title of being "the framework within which all virtue lives."[10]

Very interesting indeed is the emphasis placed on this thing called "humility" throughout the years, especially since it was unquestionably championed by Jesus himself. Why so interesting? Because in a contemporary collection of longed-for and valued traits, though spirituality is *growing* in popularity, humility might not even make the top-ten list. In popular culture there is little room for the idea of the human spirit being reliant or insufficient in its search for wholeness. The idea that there is God in some form may admittedly be gaining steam, but to suggest that this God is a personal force with specific, prescribed intentions, or that He/She/It expects humankind to give in to that "plan," is often considered too offensive (or brainless) to be true.

Sadly, though it confesses philosophical and theological "disalignment" with that offense, the Christian Church sometimes appears to act as though it were in practical agreement. Though taught to consider others as more important than ourselves, many who identify as Christians practice levels of self-absorption virtually unrivaled in all of recorded history. Invited to follow a religious leader who modeled the laying down or setting aside of one's life as the most compelling way to live, we "followers of Jesus" seem to have creatively and successfully remodeled Christianity to fit our desired lifestyles and agenda instead.

Apparently, forgiveness is only a viable option until it requires us to look weak or makes it appear as though someone has bested us. Generosity is a good thing, so long as it doesn't drain a savings account, put a comfortable retirement at risk, or require the depletion of too much personal energy. Grace is gladly received but only rarely given—especially to people with whom we disagree on selected key issues. The charge to bless the world has been somehow twisted into the freedom to dominate it. And we, the folks given the privilege of speaking the "truth in love," seem to find it difficult to remember the "love" part of the equation. Knowing doctrine is applauded more vigorously than knowing people; getting to Heaven with clean hands is of higher value than getting them dirty here in the snake-filled gardens of Earth; and being right is valued above being kind.

How do I know this with such certainty? Because I *live* it. I battle it in my own heart. And I don't think I'm all that different than most of the people I know who are hungry for a spirituality that outpaces the one they're currently experiencing.

Two popular American economists recently wrote that one of the things wrong with us in the United States is that we refuse to listen to the dead.[11] The observation they applied to our economy I also claim here for our theology. According to Teresa of Avila, John of the Cross, Thomas A. Kempis, St. Benedict, Martin Luther, the Apostle Paul, Mother Theresa, Henri Nouwen, John Wesley, Bernard of Clairvaux, Mary the mother of Jesus, and even Jesus himself, robust spirituality will only come to us through the very narrow doorway of robust humility.

Humility is not just an appendage of spiritual depth; it's the backbone of it.

Definitions of humility are difficult to quantify. In fact, the offerings of many who attempt them are either very conceptual or exclusively descriptive, listing humility's characteristics or the things that might identify it more than actually defining it. It's "accepting one's status as a dependent creature and admitting a need for the energy of God." It's "the catalyst for a realistic view of oneself."[12] Humility is "the freedom to stop trying to be what we're not, or pretending to be what we're not, and accepting our 'appropriate smallness.'"[13] Teresa of Avila is at least conceptually practical when she names humility as "the ointment for our wounds."[14] Still, these statements can feel more like references to what humility looks like or what it does than what it actually is.

I've always found it frustrating to be told how important humility is and how much I needed to acquire it without ever being given a clear and workable definition of it. It's been painfully obvious to me that I lacked it, while at the same time I've been strangely confident that without it I could never really advance in life as a spiritually well-formed man. I concluded early on that to grow in humility was going to be a painful, embarrassing, and prolonged process. I could tell it was missing in my life. But the oft-found ease of somehow sensing and recognizing its presence in others only increased my desire to acquire it for myself. I had the value and longing for humility but not the taste of it. What I lacked was a definition that would help me measure it and choose to pursue it in specific life situations.

Ironically, it was through one of those painful "life situations" that the definition I was searching for came to me. It's not a perfect definition, but it works for me because it's "provable" (in other words, it seems to make sense when applied to the life of Jesus); it's measurable (it helps me to check myself to see whether I'm practicing humility); and it's employable (I can actually apply it during the day and depend upon it to help me to make better choices.)

I'll reintroduce that definition here. HUMILITY IS THE WILLINGNESS TO BE PERCEIVED AS INSIGNIFICANT IN ORDER TO BE EFFECTIVE. It's not primarily about discipline or ability; it's about a person's compliant readiness. It's not about actually *being* insignificant, but a willingness to *appear* to be insignificant. It's not the focus; it's a hunger to let go of anything that is inclined to compete with the true focus or put it at risk. Humility is what we have when we mature to the point where efficacy trumps applause— when accomplishing an objective is of greater value than being singled out as one responsible for having accomplished it. It's getting to the level of spiritual substance where being recognized by God is actually enough; when knowing that He has noticed and nodded in approval of what He has seen is all we need. Humility is the readiness to hang on a loser's cross while knowing for certain that you are anything but a loser in the greater story.

Humility is the willingness to be perceived as common/ unnecessary/insignificant in order to be successful/faithful/ effective. And it's something that's sought and found only by the truly great, the most profoundly spiritual.

I am privileged to work with a staff of superstars at the church where I serve. Our team of unheralded part-time and volunteer workers, for instance, includes a brilliant chemist, a former teacher of the year, the very accomplished wife of a celebrated Coast Guard captain, a former rock star, a retired U.S Lieutenant Surgeon General, and more successful business owners and entrepreneurs than I can count. Each of them has contributed significantly to their families, professions, and even their country. Many have risen to the very tops of their fields. In search of human examples of humility, I really could stop with any of them. But I want to be more specific and highlight three members of our staff—three of our pastors, because to me, each of them models humility in a different way.

One of our church's pastors is older than me by about twelve years. He's been a consultant on a national scale, is by far one of the most outward-looking and compassionate people I've ever met, and has not only been the lead pastor of a church but has served on the faculty and staff of one of America's largest and most well-known seminaries. Still, he chose to leave that prestigious seminary position to come to our fellowship and become part of our modest and, at the time, struggling staff.

Since then, through his leadership, a local grammar school that was severely underfunded and underserved has gained a serious partner in our church; people are learning about God's love and being given opportunities to respond to it through our ALPHA course; adult teams of servants are being trained, then sent into challenging situations to respond to needs and help people remember that God loves them and longs to restore a friendship with them; victims of HIV/AIDS are being helped and cared for through our church's partnerships; and people are not only being provided for, but helped to escape the seemingly inexhaustible grip of poverty.

This pastor doesn't get to preach very much. And, in order to ensure that the ministry he spent three years building wouldn't suffer after financial challenges resulted in his position being cut in hours and salary, he chose (against our board's wishes and specific instructions) to keep working almost as though there had been no financial changes at all.

Being good was apparently more important to him than *looking* good. That's humility.

Our youngest associate is also our brightest strategist. By the time I've figured out how to get from point A to point B with a particular plan, he's already worked his way through the entire alphabet, with enough time left over to take his lunch break. The only "thirty-something" on our pastoral staff, when it comes to understanding and caring for "postmodern" people, he has more insight in the moment than the rest of us will have in an entire lifetime. He's incredibly popular with our people, and rates off the charts when it comes to competency in his field, but he never seems to have trouble submitting to the leadership of others when it's appropriate, and displays an insatiable appetite for learning and improving himself.

For this pastor, *contributing* to a team is a bigger deal than being recognized for it. He's the kind of person who would willfully miss a hundred team pictures for the opportunity to play in just one real game. You see, investing in the great tasks of life is more important to him than whether anyone takes note of what he contributes to them—even though, in my opinion, he's destined for greatness by just about any definition.

That's humility.

I do a big chunk of the preaching in our church, but in my

opinion, I'm not the best preaching pastor on our team. That recognition must go to a colleague who has headed up a small Bible college, has been an extraordinarily successful youth pastor, fills a classroom to overflowing any time he teaches, and is still in high demand nationally as a speaker. He would probably argue with me about both its truth and the relevance of that opening statement, but I stand by it.

He's a natural leader, has amazing abilities to discern things, and is a compassionate but courageous truth-teller. Never, though, have I sensed in him a need to be "the man." In fact, whenever I've encouraged him to be more open to official leadership positions and greater influence, his response is to remind me that he's already leading and influencing as a part of our team. I continue to remind my friend that his gifts are significant and that, in my opinion, he should be applauded for the leader he is. He keeps reminding *me* that none of that is important. What is important is that each person be given opportunities to contribute the best we can bring to our present charge in order that the people of our community might be loved, helped, and served by our church.

Our staff being configured so as to care best for people is more important to him than who is seen as its captain. That's humility.

Actually, I could write paragraphs like these about every man and woman on our team and never even come close to stretching the truth. And, contrary to popular belief, many pastors and leaders of charitable organizations (religious or otherwise) could say the same kinds of things about their colleagues. The fact is that people rarely last very long in movements that ask them to give of themselves unless humility is or is becoming a central theme in their lives. It's just that important.

Obviously, the Bible has many fine examples of humility—people who were willing to be perceived as insignificant in order to be effective. Moses was affirmed for his humility. Mary, the mother of Jesus, was heroic in her willingness to be perceived as a woman worthy of being stoned in order to give birth to the person who many, including me, would consider to be the greatest gift the world has ever known. Ruth let go of everything to give herself to her mother-in-law and put herself in a position of vulnerability in order to be claimed by a man she loved. And the whole point of Christ showing up in the first place was that he be underappreciated, underserved, under-respected, and underloved, ultimately giving up his life for the very people who took it from him. Any and all of those, plus buckets more just like them, could be cited as excellent examples of humility in the Bible.

My favorite example of someone who was willing to be perceived as insignificant in order to be effective, though, isn't on that list, even though his story isn't all that obscure. It's found in the sixth chapter of John's gospel, and it's remarkable.

Jesus was growing in popularity and huge crowds (even by today's standards) were forming to hear him teach and hopefully see him perform miracles. In John 6 we read about one of those crowds. It's in this story that I find my favorite example of the elements of humility as defined above.

Let's start at the end of the definition. There was certainly faithfulness or effectiveness in this story. Including women and children, well over five thousand people were in the crowd that followed Jesus that day. Each of them ate until they were full, with twelve baskets of leftovers gathered after everyone was finished. Feeding that many people even the simplest of meals would be a significant challenge today, with our modern kitchens and banquet halls. Jesus did it outside, on a lakeside hill, with a small staff of servers who hadn't been able to plan the meal ahead of time, and with none of our contemporary amenities. Oh, and there was no Costco nearby where he could go and purchase truckloads of food, so Jesus fed the entire horde with five rolls and two small broiled fish.

Effective in response to the crowd's need for food? Sure, but that wasn't the most impressive thing about this event. The greatest outcome of that day's expression of humility was the fact that thousands of people saw Jesus differently. He was no longer just a worker of magic tricks that made their lives easier but, as recorded in John 6:14, "the prophet who is to come into the world."

So let's recap: Jesus takes five small bread rolls and two small broiled fish and blesses them so fully that more than five thousand people are fed with them. In other words, his disciples keep walking through the seated multitude, distributing the bread and fish, but the bread and fish never run out. In fact, there are actually twelve baskets of food left over after everyone has eaten their fill.

Pretty big "wow factor," if you ask me. What's even better is that people who have previously been impressed with Jesus because of what he has done are now impressed with him because of who he is (or at least might be). As a result of eating, they have a different kind of hunger—a *spiritual* hunger.

This is not only a great miracle but also a momentous step forward for the mission of Jesus. However, an important and nagging question still remains. Humanly speaking, who is the hero of this story? Jesus, of course, but I mean who is the common villager most responsible for such a powerful display of God's ability to provide for humanity and the tendency of the human heart to long to follow the example of Christ? Who launched that?

The disciple Andrew would be a valid candidate. After all, it was Andrew who was willing to bring the basket of bread and fish to the attention of Jesus in the first place, as verses 8-9 record. "Another of his disciples, Andrew, Simon Peter's brother, spoke up, 'Here is a boy with five small barley loaves and two small fish, but how far will they go among so many?'"[15] But that depends upon how the statement is interpreted. Was he being cynical, aligning himself with the negative, "you've got to be kidding me" words of Phillip that preceded his? Or was Andrew's suggestion one of cautious, hesitant faith, as though he was saying, "This sounds crazy, but I think you have that look in your eye again, Rabbi—the one where you're testing us and you're planning to do something really wild. Could it be possible that you could actually multiply even this small lunch to the point that it feeds everyone here? But I know, I know. That's just nuts. Of course it is. What is this small basket of food for so many people?"

Either way, Jesus seemed to like the cautious, seemingly absurd baby step his young follower had taken. And, as is usually the case when Jesus sees a baby step he likes, great things happened.

But, daring as he was, I don't see Andrew as the primary hero here. I actually think it was the person who offered the food in the first place who, aside from Jesus, was the superman on this day.

We don't know for sure, so what I'm about to write is complete guesswork—nothing more than my imagination trying to come up with a context that makes sense and fills in some of the gaps of the story. But imagine a young man who had come with his family to see Jesus. His parents are somewhere in the crowd and, like everyone else, they are hungry. Not knowing what to expect but sensing that it's time to eat, and seeing that Jesus is obviously getting ready to teach or do something, Mom opens the pack that contains the food she brought with her and gives each member of her family their portion.

"Mother, may I get closer to Jesus? May I eat my lunch up the hill where my cousins are, right next to him?" Having been given permission, the boy races up to the front of the crowd and sits next to his relatives. He's excited to be close to the action. It's like sitting on the field-level rail between the bases at a Dodgers game, where you can hear everything the manager is yelling and every word the players and umpires are saying to each other (okay, not *those* kinds of words, but you get the point). Only this kid overhears a private argument between Jesus and his disciples that surprises him.

"What do you mean 'buy bread to feed them,' Jesus? There are thousands of them here. An entire year's wages would barely be enough to provide just one mouthful of bread for each person."

As I imagine it, upon hearing this and realizing what is happening, the young man looks down at his basket, then up to

Jesus, then back at his lunch again. Only a handful notice as he gets to his feet and slowly drifts away from his cousins. Coming up behind Andrew, he tugs on his robe and holds up his lunch. "Sir, I couldn't help but overhear, and I know it's not much, but will this help? My mom brought it for me, but I'll gladly contribute it if it will help to feed everyone. Maybe we could all just put our food together so everyone can have a snack. But even if you can't use it for all the people here, at least *Jesus* can have a little something to eat so he can find strength to keep teaching and doing miracles. Please tell him he can have it if he wants it."

Andrew pauses and thinks for a moment. "Only a child would be so simplistic as to think that such a big challenge could be addressed by such a small contribution. Still, my rabbi seems to delight in nothing more than shocking us by the things he does." The lad watches and listens as Andrew turns and says to Jesus, "There is a young fellow over here with five small rolls and two small fish. But what is that to so many?"

Jesus looks at the boy as he reaches for the basket. He gives him a warm, affirming but barely perceptible nod and, with eyes still locked on the new friend who brought the "ridiculously small offering," speaks to his disciples. They are good words—words that always mean something astounding is about to happen.

"Have the people sit down," he says without ever taking his eyes from the giver of the gift. Then, after an affirming wink that only he and the young donor can actually see, he continues in a near mumble intended only for those in closest proximity, "And gather the rest of our group so we can distribute this food our new young disciple has brought to us. It's well past time for us to eat."

I think this boy was the hero of this story. Furthermore, I'll argue that his heroism is an example of our definition of humility. Why? Well, because of his actions, consider the following:

- Over five thousand people were fed and introduced to a deeper understanding of the heart and agenda of Jesus.
- So impressed were the people with Jesus that day, John tells us, that they wanted to crown him king right there on the spot.
- This becomes one of the most widely known and often remembered miracles of Jesus, having been taught around the world.
- It's served as an inspiration to anyone who doesn't have an impressive résumé or bank account to offer to God, helped millions remember the beauty of childlike faith, and is the event that eventually led to Jesus's famous "I am the bread of life" statement (to the same crowd but on the other side of the lake the next day).
- This "feeding of the five thousand" has given us one of our best examples of the heart God has for the meeting of real human needs. In fact, one of the most compassionate modern efforts designed to express that heart is even called "Loaves and Fishes."

Pretty significant stuff, if you ask me. A virtual picture of effectiveness. And, aside from Jesus himself, the champion of this event and, therefore, one forever attached to its outcomes is the young person who offered his lunch—an unimpressive snack that had a *very* impressive effect.

Fine. But, you might be asking, aside from the obvious outcomes, how is this a specific example of humility as defined in this chapter? I'll answer that question with a list of additional questions. After reading about all God accomplished through his simple generosity:

1. Can anyone find the boy's name?
2. Okay then, how about his family name?
3. Does anyone know any of the specifics about where this young man of great faith, trust, and generosity was born or grew up?
4. I suggested imagined dialogue on his part, for surely he and Jesus spoke at some time. Other than his rather short statement to Andrew, can someone please direct me to any place in this story where anything he said is recorded?

Of course, the answer to all of these questions is no. And we certainly have no sense that the young fellow ran back to his cousins, siblings, or parents claiming credit for his basket being the one from which thousands were fed.

Twelve baskets of leftovers were collected after the meal, but there is no record of the boy claiming them as rightfully his (though I suspect that Jesus gave them to him and his family— another imaginative leap on my part). Reading this account, it feels almost as though the unnamed youngster handed off his meal, took several steps back, then faded happily back into the crowd, never to be heard from or referenced again.

That's humility: to be incredibly significant to the life of something marvelous, yet somehow know that recognition of your significance could come only at the cost of seeing that "something marvelous" actually happen. It's what Harry Truman reminded us of in his well-known and often-used quote: "You can accomplish anything in life, provided that you do not care who gets the credit."

Humility is that virtue that grows in us and adjusts our priorities to the point that *being* good is more important to us than *looking* good. IT'S THE WILLINGNESS TO BE PERCEIVED AS INSIGNIFICANT IN ORDER TO BE EFFECTIVE.

A prayer for those who simply must be recognized:

"Be violent and aggressive in me, oh God. Chip away at that sneaking rogue in me that is as concerned with being celebrated as it is with accomplishing anything worthy of celebration. Choke the life out of it, and in doing that prove your desire for me to really live. Create in me, Lord, what is not currently there: the ability to be at peace with anonymity. Amen."

NOTES

CHAPTER THREE
TEACHABILITY

But the three most important words in any marriage are
"Maybe you're right."

TEACHABILITY:

The Willingness to Be Persuaded By a Better Argument

D ecades after we exchanged vows on our wedding day (January 7, for those of you who want to send flowers), my wife and I still employ what turned out to be fantastic advice given to us just after we got engaged. Our friends Andy and Linda (people who have invested powerfully and sacrificially in us for most of our married lives) sat us down one day in their kitchen and said, "We're going to give you the most important three words for every marriage. Ready?"

We were, though we suspected we already knew the answer. *Everyone* knows what those three words are, right? "I Love You."

"You probably think you already know what those three words are, don't you?" Andy continued while Linda smiled. "You're thinking they are 'I love you.' Right?" We both nodded. "Wrong!"

We were shocked, and more than a little bit confused.

"Those are important words. But the three most important words in any marriage are 'Maybe you're right.'"

We used those three words a lot in the early years of our marriage, often as a warm joke, but sometimes they helped us end an argument before it ever picked up steam. Since then we've realized that what our friends were really talking about was the importance of teachability in a relationship and, more broadly, the deeply spiritual and life-giving nature of it in *any* context.

I've already included so many overused quotes in this book that I see no reason to stop now, especially when they are the words of two of my favorite celebrities and introduce my point so effortlessly. The first is from John Wooden, not only a great basketball coach but by most measures a great man. "It's what you know after you know it all that counts." And he lived long enough to know a lot, dying just a few months before his hundredth birthday.

A second quote seems philosophically connected to the first. It comes from Winston Churchill. "The most important thing about education," says Churchill, "is appetite." Can you see the connection between these two statements? Wooden is suggesting that learning is something a person must be able to do for an entire lifetime and Churchill is implying that the only possible way to live such a life is, as a popular beer commercial of the last few years suggests, to "stay thirsty, my friends."

This reminds me of an encounter I had a few years back with one of my Church History professors. It had been nearly twenty years since I'd been in his class, and I had recently been given some work assignments that made me wish I had paid better attention. In doing some of the research for those assignments I realized that I was enjoying the study a whole lot more than I ever did in school. During a break that week I saw that professor entering our lunchroom.

"Hey, Phil," I said as he walked in, "I finally figured out why I was such a mediocre student in your classes." He seemed mildly curious. "I think it was because I was being asked to eat before I was hungry. But I'm sure hungry now."

I was proof of the points Wooden and Churchill were trying to make. I had arrived at an opportunity to learn things "after I knew it all" because I was motivated by a significant appetite for learning them. I had become more teachable.

Teachability is an important component in a deep and growing spirituality. In fact, just about nothing we try to do will work very well unless we are at least moderately teachable. Jobs don't pan out, school doesn't result in much true learning, and relationships become stale, even painful when people aren't teachable. The simple fact is that teachability is crucial to just about everything we do. That's why it's an absolutely worthy addition to a list of things that describe a powerful spirituality.

I'm an Abraham Lincoln fan, but perhaps not primarily for the reasons one might think. I'm thrilled that he worked to end slavery, very much appreciate that he saw the wisdom in protecting the union of the states, love the fact that he accomplished so much in spite of the fact that he came from such palpable poverty, and am stirred every time I read one of his speeches.

Just like so many who visit it, I was left breathless the first time I visited the Lincoln Memorial and stood before his grand statue—made even more grand by the fact that it was illuminated at night. And I'm often choked up when I read

Lincoln biographies or watch documentaries about him on the History Chanel. But it isn't the fact that he was a brilliant politician, a great president, a hard worker, or the emancipator of slaves that's most compelling to me. What I love most about this president who saw value in appointing antagonists—even outright opponents—to his cabinet is the fact that he was so teachable.

I'm no Lincoln expert, not even close, but I've read enough about him to see teachabililty in just about every season of his life.

For instance, though raised by illiterate parents, he scratched out a basic education for himself. It's reported that he only had one year of formal schooling, didn't learn refined grammar until after he was twenty-one years old, and was never acquainted with basic geometry until after his fortieth birthday.[16] Still, he made a mark on history that has been equaled by few others. That just doesn't happen unless one is willing to live a life that is consumed with learning.

At the beginning of this chapter, I introduced teachability as: THE WILLINGESS TO BE PERSUADED BY A BETTER ARGUMENT. Lincoln personified this definition. Here are just a couple examples of what I mean:

Because of his meager education, Lincoln had set his sights not on being a lawyer, but a blacksmith. In his mind, the idea of ever practicing law was simply too ambitious given his meager education. But Lincoln had a few things going for him. One was a friend, the politician John Paul Stuart, who encouraged him and reasoned that he could, in fact, be a fine lawyer. The other asset Lincoln had was a willingness to listen to that friend. Though initially convinced that becoming an attorney was out of reach, Lincoln was teachable. He was willing to be persuaded by a better argument, and by 1836 he was equipped and ready for a legal career.

Among Lincoln scholars there are those who argue that from the very beginning of his campaign to be president he was an emancipationist, if not an outright abolitionist. However, that seems to be a minority view. Most writers I've read argue that his changing positions on slavery were either the result of slick political positioning or an evolution of thought. I'm convinced that the latter is true. In other words, it may have been Lincoln's teachability that led him to the gracious position he seems to have held by the time he was assassinated.[17] Note the evolution of thought, for instance, that is implied through the years in significant speeches he delivered.

In an 1858 debate with Steven Douglas, when both were candidates for the office of U.S. Senator from Illinois, Lincoln represented himself as a limited or modified emancipationist at best. In fact, many find what he said in that debate (as well as in several of his now-published letters) very disturbing. "I am not, nor ever have been in favor of bringing about in any way the social and political equality of the white and black races—that I am not nor ever have been in favor of making voters or jurors of Negroes, nor of qualifying them to hold office, nor to intermarry with white people; and I will say in addition to this that there is a physical difference between the white and black races which I believe will forever forbid the two races living together on terms of social and political equality."[18] That last statement is certainly painful to read, especially when we do so with an understanding that, from about 1850 to the early 1860s, Lincoln promoted (and even did some research regarding) the idea of establishing colonies outside of the United States for freed slaves. It was, as

I recall, to be a voluntary deportation, but at the time, some of the states' laws pertaining to freed slaves settling there made relocation (probably to South America or somewhere in the Caribbean) virtually their only viable option.

In 1861, at his first inaugural, Lincoln seems to be aiming his words at the Southern states. He's less extreme with his language, but he still seems to be holding to views they didn't teach us in grammar school when we celebrated his birthday as a national holiday. "I have no purpose, directly or indirectly, to interfere with the institution of slavery in the states where it exists. I believe I have no lawful right to do so, and I have no inclination to do so."

But Lincoln was reluctant to be forever rigid in these early held views. In fact, history shows that, once reasonably persuaded, he was willing to change his mind. According to Dr. Mark Neely, a professor of history at St. Louis University and a recognized Lincoln scholar, by 1862 Lincoln had cooled on the idea of deportation, and within two more years had dropped the idea altogether. In 1863 he went so far as to allow African Americans to serve in the Union army, effectively making a statement that they also had ownership in the nation for which they were laying down their lives. Then, in his second inaugural in 1865, Lincoln actually stated that the Civil War and all of the trials that came with it were God's punishment on America for having allowed slavery in the first place.

As noted, there are plenty who would argue (with some academic credibility) that Lincoln never truly cared at all about the slavery issue, save for its effect on his ability to keep the South from seceding. However, others contend, with at least equal force, that Lincoln actually cared a lot more than he let on—that much of what he said that we find distasteful today was the result of a political environment that would have made it impossible to win the election had he done anything else or said anything more.

But still other Lincoln scholars, Dr. Neely among them, believe that the differences in language as his speeches progressed through the years simply reflect the fact that the president changed his mind—that he heard better arguments (many from Christian abolitionist movements), saw the courage with which freed slaves, most of whom had been born in the U.S., fought to defend their country, and changed his position. That he became PERSUADED BY A BETTER ARGUMENT.

We'll probably never really know for sure what Abraham Lincoln thought on every detail pertaining to slavery, since he was a rather private man in many ways. What we can be certain of, though, is that this president who spent his entire life learning, submitted his professional plans to the wisdom and insight of accomplished friends, and, upon winning the White House, refused to fill his cabinet with "yes men," was teachable. Maybe we should all thank God that he was.

Like all of these characteristics, teachabilty is a key element to spiritual depth. That's why it's no surprise to find it in many of the Bible's most familiar champions. Here are just a handful of examples of THE WILLINGNESS TO BE PERSUADED BY A BETTER ARGUMENT:

David

The Psalms are full of the value of teachability; so is the life of the one who wrote many of them. Psalm 24:4 calls from a teachable heart, "Cause me to know your ways, Oh Lord; teach me your paths." Psalm 143:10 offers a virtual "ditto." "Teach me to do your will, for you are my God. Let your good Spirit lead me on level ground." The probable writer of those psalms certainly knew the value of teachability. In fact, he learned it the hard way.

In II Samuel 12 we have the record of a very painful "teachable moment" for King David. It's the story of the prophet Nathan "undressing" the king for his gross misbehavior—the kind of appointment with a sovereign that normally results in a beheading.

Not so with David. Even after Nathan verbally slaps David down for his adulterous relationship with Bathsheba and the murder of her loyal husband, instead of one of those weak, "I'm sorry if I've offended anyone" pseudo-apologies we're so used to hearing from professional athletes and politicians who seem to be more concerned with the fact that they were caught than that anyone might have been hurt by their actions, David is actually remorseful. He could have tried to defend what he did. Instead he realizes very quickly that his excuses would have no weight against Nathan's true and reasoned accusation. All one has to do is read Psalm 51:1-3 to see that David was repentant, receptive, and teachable.

Esther

The leveraged, positive effect of someone who will listen to insightful people and then change his or her course of action in response to what was advised has no better example than that of the Bible's Esther. "Esther" is generally thought to be a book about providence, but it could be easily argued that it's really about the power and spiritual significance of the ability to listen and learn.

The first two chapters of the book seem to be going out of their way to establish the natural level of Esther's capacity for teachability. In the few verses of chapter two that serve to introduce her, there are three references to Esther taking advice from wise people who are trying to act in her best interest. Two of those come from her uncle Mordecai, who is sharing wisdom about how she should present herself to the king (who was looking for additions to his harem and a new queen.) The other came from the eunuch who managed that harem. Each time Esther was advised, she listened. And each time she listened, it went well for her.

But these were just warm-ups for the larger stage God had reserved for Esther. Ultimately her willingness to listen and learn resulted in her being in a position to save exiled Jewish people of all ages from a cruel and unfair fate. In fact, because of Esther's teachability and the courageous, faithful things she was willing to do in response to the insights she'd gained, her people went from vanquished to vindicated—and well beyond.

Good things happen when someone is teachable. In fact, very little that is considered truly great ever happens unless someone, somewhere has learned to listen and be led, often in a direction that is very different from anything initially planned. Esther is certainly an excellent example of that.

Teachability is all over the biblical record. The Centurion of

Matthew 8 knew the importance of teachability. He confessed that he was competent at being both a leader and a follower—both teacher and student. Jesus was astounded by the faith attached to such insight, and seemed excited to be able to grant the request this Centurion brought him.

Moses learned through exhaustion that it was good to listen to the input of those wiser than he. He showed this when he listened to the advice of his father-in-law and delegated some leadership to a team of people during Israel's wandering in the desert.

Genesis 42 reveals that Joseph had obviously learned a few things between the time he was boasting about his superiority over his brothers and the time he chose to forgive them for their extreme injustice to him.

Nicodemus was a significant rabbi in Israel, but he was able to admit it when he couldn't quite comprehend something and needed help. That's why he was able to come to Jesus and ask for clarity on a few concepts. No doubt, Nicodemus' teachable spirit was probably also one of the reasons he was such an effective and respected instructor, referred to by Jesus as "the teacher of Israel."

Yes, teachability is an essential spiritual virtue, one that is embedded in virtually every major story of scripture.

Is Even *God* Teachable?

Now *there's* a question that should make some readers throw this book against the wall! What could God possibly have to learn from anyone? When would *He* ever need to be persuaded by a better argument? Wouldn't that imply that someone had a better grasp on a given situation than God? Forget the question of whether or not that *could* be true; my question is would I ever *want* that to be true, at *any* level? Answer: absolutely not. I wouldn't sleep better knowing that God had something to learn from someone.

Of course, there are those who want to imply that God doesn't know every detail of our lives, at least not until after we make decisions and actually do things. Some of those theologians are people I love and respect. Shoot, they may even be right. I just can't conceive of *how* they could be right. Best, I suppose, for us to read what they have to say and come to our own informed conclusions. For now, here are some observations I offer about teachability and the possibility that God so values it that He chooses to practice it Himself:

The Bible seems to make room for some version of the idea of God the Father and God the Son (Jesus) being at least open to being convinced. Luke 2:40 states that the child Jesus "grew in stature *and wisdom*" as he got older. Stature makes sense, but wisdom? So Jesus, the God-man, chose to be dependent upon the human teachers he came here to rescue in the first place? "God on earth" actually gained wisdom through his *experiences* on earth?

So even Jesus was teachable? Yes, but not out of divine insufficiency. God chose to experience every aspect of the human experience. In addition to being fully divine, Jesus was fully human—an example to all in humanity's otherwise flawed cohort of what is essential in life. Obviously a willingness and ability to learn and do the hard work of intellectual, emotional, spiritual, and theological development is something God wanted to model for people.

Another possible example of the teachability of Jesus is his prayer in the garden, just before his arrest. This sample is less problematic since it's God the Father he's yielding to for a better idea than the alternative Jesus is considering. "If there is another way to do this, could we choose *that* option? Is there any way you could let this cup pass from me?" That, of course, is a paraphrase of Christ's prayer, but it pretty much gives the gist. It's the prayer of a tormented soul—a man who is so disturbed that he's sweating drops of blood. But it's also the prayer of one who not only asks boldly but listens intently, and who after listening is willing to act on the better, original plan he'd already heard.

God the *Father* changing his mind, though, can *really* throw some of us for a loop. Yet that's the language the Bible uses in Exodus 32. Here's the context:

While Moses is away to receive the Ten Commandments, the people, who are left behind to wait, begin to panic. They need some kind of sign to cling to, some divine presence to reassure them that they aren't alone in the desert. So they construct an idol in the form of a golden calf and bow down to worship it. God, of course, is less than thrilled and decides to destroy the people—everyone but Moses, that is.

What happens next is astounding. Moses actually argues with God, presents a well-reasoned and compelling argument for God to choose a different option, and causes God to "change His mind." At least, that's the best language the writer of Exodus had available to describe what happened.

Question: Was this an example of God being teachable? Was he persuaded by a better argument? I can't imagine that. And it's not my intention to address the deeper issues of this biblical conundrum. Plenty of superior thinkers have done that already. What I *do* find interesting, though, is the fact that, even though Moses seems to have talked God out of destroying the people, he (Moses) then went down the mountain and orchestrated a lesser version of what he had just convinced God not to do. So what do we make of the fact that God's initial idea, or at least a modified version of it, was carried out anyway? Could it be that God was modeling some sort of "teachability" for Moses? Could it be that experiencing some level of "purposed flexibility" from God is what inspired Moses to be flexible himself?

At least three things are true in this story. First, God shows some sort of willingness to listen to the heart and logic of a human being before deciding what to do in the world. Secondly, it's very unlikely that we'll ever fully understand what's going on in God's mind when He does that (whatever "that" really is). Thirdly, this "back and forth" between God and Moses was somehow instructional to Moses, resulting in something that appears to have been some sort of a hybrid decision between partners.

My short answer to the question that introduced this section, "Is even *God* teachable?" is, "No, since there's nothing God needs to learn." But maybe a better answer is, "Yes, *even though* there's nothing he needs to learn." What seems clear here is that God is at least flexible, slowing down enough for a faithful servant to be able to keep up with Him and be involved with Him in what He's doing on earth. Even though there is no reason for God to be teachable—no situation where it will ever be possible that He could hear, much less be persuaded by a better argument—He seems enthusiastically ready to model the willingness to have one's ideas and decisions questioned by faithful partners in His cause.

Perhaps teachability is just that important to God. Maybe *the willingness to be persuaded by a better argument* is so essential to a thriving spirituality that God is willing to throw a wrench in our understanding of divine sovereignty by displaying it Himself—even though He won't and doesn't need to benefit from it.

I'll let scholars figure that one out. Gives me too much of a headache.

The list of reasons teachability is such a difficult thing to experience is probably as long as the line of people (especially leaders) who resist the practice of it. I'm one of those who struggles like that. Here are just a few of the "yeah buts" that are heard in that struggle:

1. Yeah, but teachability sometimes feels a lot like passivity.

I grew up in the days of "strong leadership." And I couldn't wait to be a practitioner. Leadership, in those days, had its best models in the corporate CEO or the combat commander. Leaders were decisive; they always knew what to do, long before anyone else could figure it out. I don't recall watching too many movies where the hero/leader had to ask the advice of anyone before making a decision. Patton was a leader, so was JFK (even though we now know that they sought advice often.) Back then, leaders were decision-makers, not decision-seekers. And I was bound and determined to lead.

Then I became a pastor and everything changed. Not my desire to lead—that remained intact. It was the *ability* to lead that seemed to be stripped from me, not the longing or intent. In a church, it seemed, a pastor had the responsibility for all the choices but none of the unencumbered freedom to make them. What churches, at least the churches I served, valued almost above all else was the right to have input in most of the common decisions, and all of the major ones. Quickly dashed were any assumptions that a sixty-year-old schoolteacher/elder would be willing and able to carry out the visions and instructions of a thirty-two-year-old, recent seminary grad. And I had very little idea what to do with that crippling reality.

I still feel somewhat guilty for the weak example of leadership I gave to the good people of my first pastorate, a new church plant in Oregon. In an attempt to figure out how to lead through consensus building, I ended up doing a lot more offending than actual leading. I now realize a big part of my problem was that I couldn't discern the difference between being teachable and being passive. And if there was anything I knew I *never* wanted to do, it was to be just another passive male.

Candidly, I had even stronger feelings about the possibility of being a passive pastor. One of my personal pastoral convictions is, "Pastor is a verb." For me, to spend time sitting in a round-table discussion group for the purpose of gaining input before pulling the trigger and doing anything significant sometimes feels more like the abrogation of leadership than the exercise of it. That's one of the reasons it's so tough to be teachable sometimes.

To be teachable implies, maybe even requires, a slower decision-making process. Being teachable demands that we take time to listen and absorb, especially since in order to be persuaded by a better argument, you have to be willing to actually *hear* the argument. It means that someone other than you might actually come up with the best idea while you appear to be inert, dependent, sitting in your chair taking notes while others make all the best contributions. And for anyone with even half an ounce of ego or passion, that's just too much to tolerate sometimes. It's one of the reasons being teachable is a relatively tough assignment: teachability feels too much like passivity.

2. Yeah, but being teachable looks like weakness.

This is a nuance of #1 above. Passivity and weakness are often mistaken for each other. Weakness is different, though, in that it centers more on appearances than feelings. Teachability feels a lot like passivity but it also *looks* a lot like weakness. And nobody wants to be perceived as a weak leader. In healthy leaders the motivation for being willing to be persuaded by a better argument is usually a genuine desire to make the best decisions for the organization being served. The problem, though, is that even when leaders *are* healthy, many of those they're serving *aren't;* and unhealthy people can mistake teachability for *inability.* They can observe a true desire to consider other ways to do something and conclude that it's little more than the kind of weakness that can't accomplish anything without others.

It's no longer the case, but when I first arrived at the church I currently serve, some of the influencers who were part of the congregation expected me to come in, take numbers, and, well, kick butt. For them, the fact that I took so much time assessing was a frustration. I was asked questions like, "You've been here a year already. Why doesn't the church have your mark on it yet?" or "What's your vision for our church and when will you begin to implement it?" (That last one is usually a trick question, by the way, one the asker often can't even explain). For them, my perceived inability to make definitive and clear changes—and to make them quickly—was a sign of weakness.

Truth be known, there was some validity to their conclusions. It's clear to me now that there was a fair amount of unrecognized weakness in me—still is, I'm sure. But what I was *actually* trying to do, best I knew how anyway, was to get a clear picture of the best direction to lead our church and the best pace at which to do it.

I was trying to learn, but I couldn't figure out how to do it fast enough for some of our congregation. Unfortunately, that looked not so much like a desire to gather understanding and make the best decision as an inability to lead because of some internal frailty.

I've since learned that the willingness to appear weak in order to ensure that the people being cared for get what they really need is actually a required strength. But it contributes to the difficulty of choosing teachability nonetheless. At least it did (and still does) in my case, because teachability looks a lot like weakness.

3. Yeah, but teachability demands that we conquer (or at least tame) our insecurities.

I can't speak for women. I'm married to one, helped to raise a pretty great one, and have many close friends that all belong to that group. But, of course, all of my life experience is from the side of being a man. And here's one thing I'm sure is true of ALL men: Every single one of us is a compilation of insecurities. The difference between a mature man and a boy dressed in a man's body, at least as I've seen life unfold, has to do not with the presence or absence of insecurities but the mastery or non-mastery of them. I suspect that this is, in some way, also true for women.

This presents something of a problem for the person who wants to go to the spiritual depth level of teachability. Why? Because insecurity is teachability's kryptonite.

Imagine the challenge of trying to acquire a virtue like teachabililty when: 1) it feels like passivity; 2) it looks like weakness; and 3) it pushes the buttons of virtually every insecurity embedded in a person's soul. The experience of teachability is essential to significant spiritual growth, but the mountain that must be conquered to find it seems unscalable. No wonder Jesus placed such enormous emphasis on a person's need to "die to self" in order to make any substantial progress in becoming more like him.

The mastery of personal insecurities and the practice of dying to oneself may be two different ways of saying the same thing. I deal more specifically with that in the chapter on celibacy, but there is some conceptual overlap here. For example, like that Centurion in Matthew 8, a secure person—even one who is a leader—has no problem being a follower as well. Insecurity, on the other hand, says that life is a competition for power, recognition, and influence. Even though we somehow know that kind of thinking to be false, we suffer from an insane addiction to its toxic wooings. Only when that insecurity is tamed or killed altogether can a man or woman know the freedom of seeing life not as a contest but as a partnership of intelligent, gifted human beings under the guidance and authority of a loving God. In other words, so long as insecurities reign, teachability can't.

British author G.K. Chesterton referred to these insecurities as a kind of madness in which we imagine the whole world revolves around us and we constantly fear what others think of us. "But how much happier you would be if you only knew that these people cared nothing about you!" he wrote. "How much larger your life would be if your self could become smaller in it. . . . You would break out of this tiny and tawdry theatre in which your own little plot is always being played, and you would find yourself under a freer sky, in a street full of splendid strangers."[19]

Unfortunately, there is no such thing as an insecurity that dies easily. To recognize and expose them can be both embarrassing and debilitating. But, as Chesterton promised, the results and rewards are well worth the pain, because they include the peace that finds root in a life not consumed with always being the hero of every story and giver of every answer. That's a peace that always attends a teachable spirit.

Why is teachability so difficult to find and maintain? Because it requires us to stir up the silt of our insecurities, to actually wrestle with them. And it's just a lot easier—in the short term, anyway—to leave them undisturbed.

4. Yeah, but teachability makes you vulnerable to your enemies.

I've come to the conclusion that every Popeye has his Brutus. Every life and situation is stocked with opportunistic bullies.

Whether a person works for a church or an insurance company, is trying to cure cancer or get the best deal on a new set of tires, they will most likely encounter someone who feels that his or her purpose in life is to trip them up. I suppose that's just one of the many unfortunate expressions of human brokenness. And it's all around us.

Jesus knew this firsthand. After all, the religious leaders who opposed him most vehemently were actually supposed to have spent their lives helping people get ready to receive him. And wasn't Judas in his close circle of friends? It was, in part, Christ's determined commitment to always act in the best interest of the very people who were so fickle toward him that made him vulnerable. Teachability does that. Teachability makes possible some of life's most fulfilling personal encounters, but because it must, by its very nature, employ the risks of trust and openness, it also exposes the heart to the most vicious and well-camouflaged of saboteurs.

That's teachability's potentially fatal flaw. Commit yourself to teachability and you will be vulnerable to being wounded by those who appear to live only for an opportunity to place you in their crosshairs. Yet the teachable person, fully aware of the fact that he or she is the target of unknown enemies masquerading as allies, walks knowingly and vulnerably as an uncomfortable but willing target. For them, teachability (and the spirituality it points to) is a worthy endeavor. Yes, it's one that makes a person vulnerable to enemies, but it's also one by which those very enemies will eventually be overcome.

Teachability is definitely not an easy journey, but any expedition in search of a healthy spirituality will fail without it. It's just that important.

Throughout history, this discipline or virtue of teachability has been a critical asset to those who have sought to live effective lives. Harry Hopkins, key advisor to President Roosevelt, was not initially in favor of the United States getting involved in the European struggle that eventually became World War II. He was willing to listen to FDR about the potential dangers of U.S. passivity, though—especially after the fall of France and the realization that England (and possibly Russia) stood alone in the battle against Nazi Germany.

Then, amid strong congressional pressure to minimize the potential effectiveness of Churchill and deny England the support she was requesting, [20] Hopkins traveled to the U.K., where he was heavily briefed by Churchill. As a result of that meeting, Hopkins became persuaded that an investment in Churchill's leadership would be a good idea.

In fact, Hopkins even quoted from scripture when, in a toast at a small dinner party before his departure back to the States, he informed Churchill of his intent to recommend U.S. aid. "I suppose you wish to know what I am going to say to President Roosevelt on my return. Well, I am going to quote to you one verse from the Book of Books: 'Whither thou goest, I will go and where thou lodgest I will lodge, thy people shall be my people, and thy God my God.'"

Hopkins, like the president he represented, was not without his convictions. He was opinionated, clear-thinking, well organized, and quite active as an advocate for the poor and hurting. But he was also something all great souls still are. Thankfully, Hopkins was teachable.

Teachability is *THE WILLINGNES TO BE PERSUADED BY A BETTER ARGUMENT.* It's a characteristic not of the most pathetic and wobbly of hearts, but the most virile and sure—the mark not of a spirituality that is feeble, but of one that's robust. It's crucial and far too rare. So, no matter the force or cunning of the temptation to do so, teachability is something over which no seemingly good reason to abandon it should ever be allowed to hold sway.

At all costs, let us be teachable.

A prayer for the inflexible:

"Lord, I can't see what my eyes aren't open to, and I can't acknowledge what my ears refuse to hear. If I'm honest, this chapter smacks not so much of teachability as indecisiveness. Will You show Your mercy by showing me the difference? And will You eradicate the pride that keeps me from valuing any idea that didn't originate from my own brain? I would appreciate that . . . and so would those who trust me to lead them. Amen."

NOTES

CHAPTER FOUR
CELIBACY

Celibacy has been primarily and foundationally about the putting down of compulsions.

CELIBACY:

*The Willingness to Kill Every Impulse that Needs to Die
(or corral it if it insists on living)*

D on't panic. By including a chapter on celibacy in a book about substantial spirituality, I'm not suggesting that we return to the practice of sexual abstinence among clerics, forbidding intimate encounters between a husband and wife who may be assigned the role of serving communion on the coming Sunday, or annulling the otherwise legitimate marriages of clergypersons upon ordination. All of this and more has, at different times in Christian history, been practiced. Some of it still is. But that certainly isn't the point of this chapter.

Nor is it my desire, however, to altogether remove the idea of sex from the concept of celibacy. That would be ridiculous. In fact, in a recent conversation with one of the members of our church I was put in a situation where I had to gently but faithfully remind him that Christian standards hadn't changed. To be sexually active outside of the context of marriage is still considered a sin, even for a forty-two-year-old divorced man who hasn't been called upon to struggle through the practice of self-imposed sexual abstinence for over twenty years.

I'm simply attempting to look behind the term "celibacy" to see what else might be connected with it, especially insofar as those things might be part of the realization of a lasting and more profound spirituality. I'm arguing that it may be time to take the discussion of celibacy beyond the exclusive context of sexual practice, all the way to the issue of the impulses that guide, drive, torture, and in too many cases define so much and so many of our lives.

Celibacy is, at its core, the practice of self-denial. Yes, it was originally the practice of denying oneself the privilege of a spouse and the comfort of being surrounded by a family. And yes, it's now understood to refer almost solely to the allegedly unnatural practice of not engaging in sexual activity (more about all that later). But in every case, celibacy has been primarily and foundationally about the putting down of compulsions (whether natural, unnatural, good, bad, or morally neutral) that did not serve a desired or stated goal.

What this chapter is suggesting goes well beyond recapturing the medieval or original definition of celibacy. In fact, it's pretty close to being a *re*definition of it. But when we're talking about deep spirituality, we're talking, at least as far as "celibacy" is concerned, about expanding our understanding—realizing that even though celibacy obviously addresses sexual activity, it is about *more* than that. CELIBACY IS THE WILLINGNESS TO KILL EVERY IMPULSE THAT NEEDS TO DIE, OR CORRAL IT IF IT INSISTS ON LIVING.

Don't get me wrong here. By writing this, I'm not claiming to have arrived. There are still far too many instances of me indulging unhealthy urges—opening the crypts and cages that usually contain them and offering secret furloughs that never result in anything good. But with increasing regularity, something good is happening when my most rotten compulsions seek to align themselves for a temporary yet still unfriendly takeover of my heart. More and more, a deeper, more ample spirituality is flexing its muscle. It's a spirituality of fatal hostility toward things that have no ability to do good for my soul (or the souls of others, for that matter). It's one that understands that the fact that something might feel good doesn't necessarily mean it actually *is* good. This spirituality seeks the demise of every impulse that needs to die, or at least its incarceration if it refuses to die. And in experiencing it, I'm rediscovering a *new* celibacy.

As stated in the opening paragraphs of this chapter, I'm convinced that, even though the face of "celibacy" has been changing for centuries, it's probably due for yet another facelift. In other words, it may be well past time for us to admit that the practice needs to look different today than it has in the past—including expanding its meaning to include but go beyond sexual abstinence.

Though to take the idea of celibacy beyond a discussion of sexual activity may seem foreign and new to some readers, to many in religious history—especially in the East—it never *has* been so narrowly understood or defined. In fact, the word "celibacy" has experienced quite an interesting evolution of meaning and usage through the centuries. So who's to say its meaning couldn't (or shouldn't) keep morphing and expanding?

"Celibacy" comes from a Latin word meaning "single" or "unmarried." Any ancient mention of a celibate person was specifically a reference to an unmarried person. What the word has evolved to mean in most usages today is actually more accurately represented by the words "continence" or "chastity," both of which speak of deliberate sexual abstinence more than marital standing. So originally celibacy spoke not so much of one's sexual activity as it did of one's marital status, while chastity spoke not of one's marital status but of one's sexual activity.[21] A person, then, could be celibate but not chaste (meaning unmarried yet sexually active) or chaste but not celibate (not sexually active yet married).

The fluctuating usage of the word "celibate" continued to the point that, by the early fourth century, it had come to describe not an unmarried person but a married person who was not having sex with his/her spouse. So in that case, "celibate" meant not "unmarried" but, in fact, the opposite, completely absorbing the meaning of "chaste" and jettisoning the idea of being "single" altogether.

Add to this the fact that in casual conversation today the word "celibate" and the original sense of the word "chastity" are used synonymously. In other words, a common contemporary discussion about a person who is "celibate" and a person who practices "chastity" is usually understood to be a discussion about a person (whether married or not) who chooses to live a life void of sexual activity of any kind.

Completely descriptive and open to contributions by just about anyone, TheUrbanDictionary.com is a sort of underground record of slang and common word usage. It's an attempt to record "the language of the street," and I love it for the way it reflects such a raw, popular understanding of things. For me, it's a good way to map the meanings people are currently ascribing to different words (not to mention what my kids mean when they use words in ways I've never heard them used before). I read a post on this site about the difference between chastity and celibacy, and in it a colorful, amusingly insightful person writes simply that "chastity means no sex while you are single. Celibacy means no sex while you are breathing."

Even though this contributor is a bit "bottom-line heavy" with this statement, he or she does make a point of trying to distinguish between chastity and celibacy. In so doing, we're given a pretty clear picture of how the common and assumed meaning has shifted over the centuries and continues that shift today. Now it's "chastity" that has to do with marital status and "celibacy" that has the more global, severe application. A complete reversal in usage has occurred.

The popular and functional meaning of words, and therefore the understanding of the concepts attached to them, is flexible; it's a moving target. So it makes sense that our understanding of celibacy has been evolving for some time and is still in the process of morphing. Is it historically about sex? Sure it is—just like marriage is about sex. But like marriage, celibacy is also about much *more* than sex. It's been changing faces almost since the first time it was introduced as an idea. And it's past time for it to receive a much-needed update.

As Gabrielle Brown puts it in her book, *The New Celibacy,* "Thus celibacy is not to be thought of as mere abstinence from sex, for that is what we all do most of the time anyway (at least most of us do). But it is more accurately understood as a conscious choice made on the behalf of one's greater personal gain."

Actually, celibacy is seen by many as much more than a harsh restriction.

In his book *Celibacy: Means of Control or Mandate of the Heart?*, author Michael Crosby deals with the issue of the Catholic Church requiring that priests be both unmarried and sexually inactive. One of the things he suggests is the need to broaden and deepen our understanding of the discipline of celibacy, even referring to it as a form of fasting. In other words, he implies that celibacy is one among many types of self-denial for the purpose of spiritual gain. It's best understood, he argues, not as a spiritual prohibition but a spiritual discipline.

In the Eastern Christian tradition it's argued that all Christians (not just priests) are doing their souls a favor to involve themselves in the practice of celibacy. For people of that tradition, the idea of celibacy (meaning sexual abstinence in this case) is tied not so much to the priesthood as to monasticism and, more specifically, asceticism. And since the Eastern Christian Church emphasizes the monastic and ascetic as normal streams for *every* life, this celibacy (albeit practiced for short seasons and in small doses) is something that can contribute to the spiritual health of every person—even a married person. So in this context, celibacy is about both sex and self-denial.

Eastern Orthodox priest Father Maximos Davies writes, "The ascetic realizes that what other people give him/her by way of love finds its true and deeper meaning in the One who is the source of all love. Celibacy is the practical recognition of the reality that lies behind the image, of the prototype behind the icon. Human love without celibacy is at best mere sentiment, at worst a form of idolatry."[22] In other words, and much more generally stated, celibacy is not primarily about *sexual* substance but *spiritual* substance; it's ultimately connected not so much to conjugal intimacy as to spiritual depth.

That idea of celibacy being tied more broadly to self-denial (and therefore substantial spirituality) than merely to sexual activity (and, specifically, the absence of sex) is furthered by Father Davies when he writes: "Christian celibacy is marriage baptized. Christian celibacy is the revelation of the presence of the Kingdom of God in every relationship. It is the refusal to see other people as things to be used even for the sake of romantic love. Celibacy means the willingness to see in sexuality not something merely animal, or simply useful or enjoyable, but instead something mystical."[23] And while Davies admits that he's applying to "celibacy" a "very general meaning," he is convinced that it's a more useful and accurate one.

But this broader understanding of the value and purpose of celibacy as spiritual discipline isn't limited to the Christian world. In Buddhism the practice of sexual abstinence is primarily about the development of character. In Hinduism it's a discipline that serves the deeper purpose of helping people focus on the divine. Even in the ancient world of philosophy, celibacy as sexual abstinence was sometimes practiced for the purpose of protecting and promoting a more clear-headed approach to philosophy and reason.[24] And contemporary psychology is even trumpeting the life-altering benefits of asexuality and a life without sexual activity.[25]

So what's the point of all these details and examples? When it comes to spirituality, I'm arguing (along with so many others) that celibacy is essential to any dynamic practice of it. Instead of being limited in scope to deal only with the issue of chastity, then discarded as irrelevant, celibacy should be clothed in new, more expansive meaning (which is actually not that new at all) that includes but is not limited to chastity, then re-embraced as a valuable spiritual discipline.

Celibacy is ultimately about dying to self. It's about inviting and allowing God to deal harshly with any urge that mitigates the process of being conformed to and aligned with the dream He has for all of creation. It's the willingness to kill every impulse—sexual or otherwise—that needs to die (or corral it, if it insists on living). And it is foolish to assume that we can ever experience any meaningful level of spiritual depth without the reacquisition and serious practice of it—whether it involves the practice of sex or not.

Key in the life of Jesus (and any good leader throughout history, for that matter) is the practice of celibacy as defined here in this chapter. Good leaders understand and employ the practice of denying themselves anything that detours them from their goal. Jesus (and his followers after him) modeled and taught that form of celibacy as a dominant theme. So I find it curious that the theme of self-denial or the practice of "dying to self" (both of which are terms synonymous with the biblical concept of self-control) aren't more prevalent in popular Christian thinking and teaching today, at least here in America.

Here are some examples of just how pervasive this teaching of celibacy is to the heart of the faith with which I align myself:

The Apostle Paul and His Apostolic Colleagues

The Apostle Peter (in II Peter chapter 1) mentions "self-control" as one of the important building blocks to love, which is the ultimate expression of any religion. James emphasizes the importance of "controlling" one's tongue and curbing one's speech. The writer of Hebrews writes passionately about a long list of people who "denied themselves" in profound and painful ways in Hebrews 11 and 12. And in his letters, the Apostle John encourages the discipline of resisting practices he identifies as being aligned with what he calls "the boastful pride of life."

So Paul wasn't the only apostle to champion the idea of celibacy as housed in the term "self-control." He was, however, the most prevalent. Probably since he wrote the majority of the New Testament letters that comprise our Bible, apart from Jesus himself, Paul has the most to say about celibacy as "self-denial" or "dying to self."

In Acts 24 Luke records Paul's conversation with Felix and his wife, Drusilla. In that conversation Paul emphasizes three things: righteousness, self-control, and coming judgment. I find it interesting that self-control (something that I've already noted gets far too little attention these days) is sandwiched between "righteousness" and "coming judgment," two topics that most would identify as *major* themes in current Christian rhetoric. Apparently Paul saw the willingness to put down unhelpful urges as something important enough to Christian spirituality to be included when he discussed the Christian faith with influential people.

I Corinthians is a letter *full* of references and inferences to this expanded understanding of celibacy. Two of the most obvious appear in the seventh chapter, where Paul is addressing issues of marriage and sex. Worth noting is the beginning of the chapter, specifically verses 1-9. In verse 5 Paul seems to be addressing something that was a normal practice then: temporary sexual abstinence among married couples. He implies that this is a good thing since it can contribute to spiritual depth by somehow nourishing a more substantial prayer life. But by verse 9 he's also offering a warning against pushing this practice (of sexual abstinence in a marriage) too far. More importantly for our discussion, in doing this he ties the idea of temporary marital chastity to the concept of self-control. So our contemporary concept of celibacy (which, again, is synonymous more with the word "chastity" in Paul's world) is linked very firmly with the idea of "dying to self" or self-control.

Then, in chapter 9 of the same letter, Paul lets on that his practice of celibacy (as self-denial) is crucial to his ability to maintain integrity and grow in maturity. "I buffet my body," he writes, "so that I won't say one thing and then prove to be unable to do what I teach others to do."

Earlier in the chapter he references the right to bring a wife along with him on his mission (as did some of the other apostles when they traveled) and the right to receive remuneration for his work. In both instances, Paul chose to put aside those rights for the sake of greater effectiveness in his task. He compares this form of self-denial to the disciplines of an athlete, even going so far as to call his sacrifices "my reward," much in the same way a runner links the pain of severe workouts with the joy of crossing the finish line ahead of the pack.

Is Paul clearly referring to our modern understanding of "celibacy" with his every expression of personal sacrifice? Hardly.

But by including the idea of going without a wife as a traveling companion and choosing to forfeit pay he deserves for his work when he travels, it sure does sound like he at least links the practice of sexual abstinence and nonsexual forms of self-denial under the same banner.

There simply is no question that celibacy—the willingness to kill every impulse that needs to die (or corral it if it insists on living)—played a major role in the life and teachings of the apostles, especially Paul.

Jesus and the Celibate Life

Celibacy as "dying to self" is so deeply woven into the mission and life of Jesus that it almost seems unnecessary to point it out. But given the way we tend to pursue spirituality while neglecting the idea of self-denial, a few examples should probably be given anyway. These will come in the form of a harsh conversation with Peter, a challenge to all Christian disciples to spend life "on a cross of our own," a direct encounter with Satan, and a Pauline observation of what Jesus actually "died to" in favor of coming to Earth to "die again."

First, that harsh, even painful and embarrassing conversation with Peter:

The sixteenth chapter of Matthew contains a fairly well-known affirmation of the Apostle Peter. Jesus asks a question about who his followers think he really is and Peter gives a great answer, stepping out to claim that Jesus is actually the Messiah for which they have all been looking. This is followed by a pretty substantial "attaboy" from Jesus, who not only claims that God himself spoke through Peter's words but renames him "Rock" and promises to, in some way, build the church on Peter's ministry.

But Christ's affirmation is sandwiched between two rebukes, one of which is aimed specifically at the newly named "Rock" himself. The personal rebuke in question gives insight into what Jesus believes it takes to be a true follower of his teachings. Not surprisingly, it focuses on Peter's unwillingness to accept the fact that part of what Jesus (and later Peter himself) must do in order to be faithful to his mission is (either effectively or literally) die. When Jesus reveals that he must go to Jerusalem and suffer, Peter is beside himself, even though Jesus predicted not only his death but also his resurrection.

"Not on my watch!" Peter announced. "I forbid allowing this to happen." Christ's response reveals his thinking on the centrality of "celibacy" or self-denial to mature spirituality.

"When you think like that," Jesus essentially says, "your thoughts are antithetical to the thoughts of God." In other words, Peter wanted to avoid death and dying to self while God wanted to pursue it.

But this doesn't stop with Jesus rebuking Peter for not endorsing his plan to suffer and die. From there Jesus goes on to explain that, for his followers, the self-denial of celibacy— even in the extreme—is absolutely normal and to be expected. "Unless you are willing to die to yourself daily, take up your cross, and follow me [in going to the cross for this cause of ours], you are not worthy to be called my followers." If celibacy is essentially the willingness to kill every impulse that needs to die (even when that impulse is an insuppressible need to live), then this is a clear example of Christ's quest for celibacy.

Earlier, in the fourth chapter of Matthew, we see another expression of Jesus's familiarity with self-denial. This time, though, he encounters not his followers but his enemy. Vulnerable, hungry, alone, and exhausted, Jesus finds himself in the wilderness, face to face with Satan himself. Opportunist that he is, Satan takes advantage by tempting Jesus to cave in to some of humanity's deepest longings: 1) the longing for physical satisfaction; 2) the longing to be recognized as special; and 3) the longing for power. But actually there was more to Satan's wooings, for he was ultimately tempting Jesus to avoid something painful, embarrassing, even fatal. He was enticing him to take a detour around the cross.

Fortunately, Jesus understood what was going on and stayed committed to a life of celibacy. He was in touch with the connection between spirituality and self-denial. He was willing to say no to stopping his own temporary pain in favor of eventually being able to say yes to stopping the eternal pain of others. The true celibate always thinks like that; and Jesus was a true celibate.

John 15 records a less spectacular but no less important example of a celibate lifestyle. Jesus announces that "the greatest expression of love that anyone can have is to lay down his or her life for a friend." The important question for our purposes here revolves around what it means to "lay down one's life." Obviously, this could include the idea of experiencing physical death for friends, as was ultimately the case with Jesus. But there is also the less dramatic but more often called-for sense of *setting aside* one's life (or agenda) for one's friends. This too is a dying to self and, thus, an expression of celibacy as we're defining it. It's a killing of the compulsion to put yourself ahead of all others. And Jesus presents it as a critical mark of the celibate life.

Our final example of celibacy in the life of Christ actually comes in a text written by the Apostle Paul while describing Jesus. In the second chapter of Philippians, Paul is challenging Christ-followers to adopt the attitudes and practices of Jesus. Then he names the specifics. Jesus, though deserving of recognition as God, didn't consider that recognition and position to be something to cling to—especially when the alternative was service to others. So what he did was to "empty himself," both of the experience of being universally recognized as divine and even of some of the functions and prerogatives of divinity. Jesus seems to have died (at least temporarily) to the need to be worshipped in order to bring freedom to those held captive by *their own* need to be worshipped. He voluntarily let go of power in order to give hope to those who were grasping for it. He took on the form and function of a humble servant in order to give real life to people who were blinded by a perpetual and unhealthy preoccupation with being served.

Philippians chapter 2 is a major theological passage. There's a lot there that could be easily missed. One thing that it's impossible to miss, however, is the fact that the cost of all of this "life-giving" is the multifaceted death (or lifetime of "deaths") of the one who seeks to give it.

Celibacy is *the willingness to kill every impulse that needs to die (or corral it if it insists on living).* And by this definition, Jesus was nothing if not a celibate.

Surprisingly, not all examples of celibacy in this expanded sense are ancient. Believe it or not, they are increasingly common in pop culture too.

My friend Doug is also one of my favorite thinkers and teachers, so when he suggests that I read a book or see a movie, I generally get right on it. But to read the book he was recommending this time seemed ludicrous. It was a vampire book—and not just ANY vampire book, either. This was a book about adolescent vampires (well, vampires presenting as adolescents, anyway).

Really? Was my high-functioning, intellectual friend beginning to slip? Not only did I have no interest in reading the book, I was also tempted to quit reading this particular issue of his blog. However, because of who this was and how often he surprised me with his insights, I decided to give in. Boy was I glad I did.

It turned out that the book Doug was writing about, which was outrageously popular among adolescents and young adults, had as a major theme the idea of celibacy—even *our* idea of it as presented in this chapter.

Bella (the protagonist) and Edward (the hundred-and-four-year-old vampire living as a high school student) fall in love. But Edward is a different kind of vampire in a different kind of vampire family. He, along with his parents and siblings, puts down his urge to consume human blood in favor of the blood of wild animals. In other words, he says no to what for him are very natural longings because of the damage acting on them would do to others.

But Edward doesn't stop at redirecting his lust for human blood. No, he also puts down a strong adolescent compulsion for sexual intercourse with Bella. Why? Because to engage her in that much intimacy could put her at risk of his bite, robbing her of her humanity (in the story, receiving the bite of a vampire causes you to *become* one) and making for her a life-altering decision. It's a decision he feels she is not ready to make and one that he certainly feels he has no right to make *for* her. In spite of Bella's oft-expressed desire to be sexually involved with Edward, and convinced that those longings come more from her natural attraction to him than any informed desire to choose the vampire's life for herself, Edward refuses Bella's advances. His own physical desire for Bella doesn't disappear. In fact, it continues its typical teenage crescendo. Still, he curbs his very strong impulses and acts in what he feels is Bella's best interest instead.

When asked about this abstinence theme in her writing in the April 2008 issue of *Time Magazine*, author Stephanie Meyer said, "The books are centered around Bella's choice to choose her life on her own, and the Cullens' [that's Edward's family name] choices to abstain from killing rather than follow their temptations. I really think that's the underlying metaphor of my vampires. It doesn't matter where you're stuck in life or what you think you have to do; you can always choose something else. There's always a different path."

Whatever our opinions about Meyer's work, we must acknowledge that she's correct about at least one thing: regardless of where we're stuck in life or which compulsion seems to be sticking us there, there is always a different path. There is always a different choice we can make in response. We can seek to kill any impulse that needs to die or corral it if it insists on living. We can choose celibacy—sexual or otherwise.

A second example of this expanded view of celibacy in popular culture comes from a film that was released in 2001, based on the book from which the film took its name, *A Beautiful Mind*. This is the story of John Forbes Nash Jr., a Princeton mathematician and Nobel laureate. It's also the story of his battle with paranoid schizophrenia and the "appearances" of people and voices that weren't really there, except in his own head. I won't go into the details of the film, but I consider it a worthy investment of time—not surprising, since it won the Academy Award for best picture that year.

What I find compelling in a conversation about celibacy is the way the film tracks Nash's struggle with and against the manifestations of his disease and, more specifically, the practice of isolating and disarming the "voices" he was hearing. The accuracy of the film in portraying the actual historical details isn't as important to my point as the message Hollywood is sending in the artistic rendering of the story itself. In fact, much of what the movie presents is false at worst and embellished at best. But this film is more "statement of hope" than "presentation of facts," more dream than documentary. In fact, the scene from which I make this point (the Princeton pen ceremony) is based on something that probably never even took place. Still, it portrays a compelling and heartfelt story of celibacy insofar as celibacy can be assigned the definition I'm suggesting.

In "The Pen Ceremony" scene, Nash (Russell Crowe) is sitting with a member of the Nobel Committee, who is seeking assurances that Nash will be emotionally healthy enough to receive the Nobel Prize (he shared the 1994 prize for economics with two others) without embarrassing the selection committee or infringing upon the elegance of the ceremony. The dialogue between the two, which occurs just before each of Nash's colleagues ceremoniously presents him with a personal pocket pen, is quite insightful.

Nash's character begins, "You came here to find out if I was crazy? If I would screw everything up if I actually won . . . dance around the podium stark naked and squawk like a chicken, things of this nature?"

"Something like that, yes."

"Would I embarrass you? Yes, it is possible. You see, I . . . I *am* crazy. I take medications, but I still see things that don't exist. I just choose not to acknowledge them. I *choose not to indulge certain appetites.*"

It's those last two lines that cause the bells to ring in my mind—especially that final line. "I choose not to acknowledge them. I choose not to indulge certain appetites." This is a wonderful expression of the very practical approach to celibacy that I'm so keen for us to reclaim and redeploy in any pursuit of a vital spirituality. Whether sexual, delusional, representative of a hunger for power, or an attempt to compensate for some overwhelming expression of a dominant insecurity, the apprehension of a prevailing spirituality will always depend upon the ability to "*choose not to indulge certain appetites.*" It will always require significant facility with the often painful but determined ability to say no to every craving that serves only to detour us. It must always find an ability to deny both voice and privilege to each and every unsavory or unproductive desire.

Celibacy says what Russell Crowe's character said to those phantom, lying voices, "Die or be forever silenced." For it is

THE WILLINGNESS TO KILL EVERY IMPULSE THAT
NEEDS TO DIE, OR CORRAL IT IF IT INSISTS ON LIVING.

All the children of my young years had a huge, furry friend. He would show up in the commercials of our Saturday morning cartoon shows speaking in the deep yet comforting voice of a local radio disc jockey. He always had the same message: "Remember, only *YOU* can prevent forest fires."

Though a more logical response might have been intimidation, all the kids on my block *loved* Smokey the Bear. With shovel in hand, his soothing baritone voice, confident smile, and familiar park ranger hat somehow worked in harmony to produce a sort of hypnotic loyalty in us, along with a deep sadness at the thought that people could actually be careless enough to burn down the acres of beautiful trees, vegetation, and habitat that served as Smokey's home. Even today, as I approach the end of my sixth decade of life, the thought of Smokey asking me to help him keep our forests green and our animals safe rouses a warmth in my heart and an almost robotic response. "Yes," I still answer silently, "I will do everything within my power to prevent such tragedy. You can still count on me, Smokey."

I mention this at the conclusion of a chapter about celibacy because of a particular experience I had in the mid-sixties as my dad, brother, and I hiked into Sayles Canyon and the Bryan Meadow campground, which had served as the high sierra base for our dad's annual hunting trip for more than twenty years. Still too young to be included in the actual hunt that would come weeks later, my younger brother and I were always excited to walk in on Labor Day weekend to repair and restock the remote wilderness camp our dad (and older uncles before him) had carved out for themselves and improved each subsequent year.

Once we had arrived at camp, our first jobs were to clear the area of new brush, pitch tents, and collect firewood for the campfire. Then it was on to something that always amazed my brother and me: the gathering of the pots, pans, and leftover canned food that had been stashed the previous year. They were always under the same rock, near the same stream, in the same burlap sack. Some of those frying pans had been in that camp since the first year my old great-uncles had established it. I could tell that the unearthing of them each year was something of a sacrament for my dad, as though the rediscovery of each cooking utensil was also a reconnection with the men with whom he had shared this annual pilgrimage in years past but could do so only in his heart from now on—men like his brother Mario, killed in a plane crash, and friend Dick Lyon, who had gone to sleep watching a golf match on the couch while his wife cooked dinner and never awoken.

"Your uncle Mario built this grill in '61," he would say as he lifted a large rock and revealed a crude, heavy stovetop around which a stone enclosure would later be built for cooking and warmth. Then, ramping up from a chuckle to a full-blown laugh and pointing to the black-and-white animal we used to pack our load in and out for most of the years I was involved with the trip, he added, "and that jackass hauled it all the way in here on his back. I thought your uncle was going to shoot old Blackjack the year he laid down in a stream and tried to dump the whole load halfway here. I mean, Uncle Mario actually had his sidearm drawn and was calling Jack every name in the book—some I hadn't ever heard before. Good thing I stopped him or we'd have had to carry everything the rest of the way on *our* backs."

Then, with his voice trailing off and his face shifting to that look people get when their eyes are open but it's obvious they're focusing more on something in their minds than on anything they're actually looking at, he added, "And I do believe he'd have done it, too."

"And Uncle Mario built this just for our camp?" I asked.

"Yep. Your uncle was really something," he said, as he seemed to stare into the nonexistent eyes of the hastily constructed iron grill. "I can't come here without thinking of him."

It was at moments like this that I realized just how special the place was to my father and my uncles. They loved that wilderness area, and they were quite impatient with anyone who did things to harm it. Maybe that was why we stopped each year at one place in particular on the hike into camp for a lecture I could almost recite verbatim every time my dad delivered it.

"Let's take a break here," Dad would say each year at the exact same spot on the trail. "Tie off the horses and let's rest in the shade." The problem, though, was that there *was* no shade where Dad had stopped. Years earlier a hiker's campfire had gotten out of control, burning hundreds of acres of forest. Ashen silhouettes of trees that once offered protection, housing, and beauty were all that remained, and Dad meant to use them to illustrate a point he made year after year during this annual work trip.

He was making Smokey Bear's point, to be sure, but though he didn't realize it, he was also illustrating the point of this chapter.

"Can you imagine that fire raging up this hill?" he would ask as he pointed up the mountain, the obvious direction the fire had traveled. Then he asked the same question he had put before us the previous year and the year before that. "Do you know what it took to eventually put out this fire? Airplanes, tractors, hundreds of people risking their lives, and God only knows how much money. But do you know the best way to put out a fire like that?"

We nodded, because we actually *did* know the answer. How could we *not* know it, with him drilling it into us every year at this same spot?

"That's right," he lectured, "the best way to put out a forest fire is to blow it out while it's still just a lit match. Do *that*," he said, before pointing at the sad, blackened remains of the once-beautiful pines that no longer offered shade as they lined our resting spot, "and you'll never do *this*."

Our dad was offering a lesson about the destructive potential of something that was designed to give warmth and life—a caution about a flame's propensity to warm you one day and betray you the next. But his memorable and practical advice is also a fitting conclusion to this chapter on celibacy. For celibacy essentially has to do with the wise use of restraint. Celibacy is the careful use of an open flame. It's making sure that a "match" designed to protect and enhance your life isn't allowed to become the agent that consumes it.

When I think of celibacy I think of our camp's fire, enclosed with large stones in order to contain the flames and capped with Uncle Mario's cooktop and screen to limit the formation of floating embers. I consider the way we took care to stack firewood at a safe distance, and the extra trouble we went through to stir and restir the life out of its already water-soaked ashes every time we left the camp. But mostly I recall resting on that trail and gazing upon hill after hill of once majestic timbers, now little more than deformed, hunchbacked reminders of what they once were, forever disabled by a single match that ignited a seemingly harmless stray twig, that rolled onto a small pile of dry pine needles, that was blown in five different directions by impassioned winds, and eventually broke out into a full-blown disaster that would take generations to repair itself.

Celibacy is the decision to put out the fire while it's still a match. It's *the willingness to kill every impulse that needs to die (or corral it if it insists on living).* And without it, spirituality will never take deep root.

A prayer for those who feel powerless against their compulsions:

"Honestly, God, this is an impossible prayer. It's one for which I have little or no faith, but an abundance of frustration and confusion. Kill these urges in me? Corral them? I've failed so often that I'm almost convinced that You authored them—that You PROLONG them in me. So if they are to die, it must be YOU who smothers them—YOU who squishes them—YOU who snuffs them out. Help me, dear, holy assassin. For if You don't, I fear I'll nourish those inner drives to the point where THEY kill ME. Amen."

CHAPTER FIVE
COURAGE

Courage is the divine seed that resides somewhere deep in all of us and competes with fear for its rightful place at center stage.

COURAGE:

The Willingness to Make Sure that Fear Never Dictates Actions

C ourage is a virtue that's difficult to define. But we sure do know it when we see it. Vicki Soto never saw herself as a hero. The twenty-seven-year-old was most at home in the classroom, where her greatest joy was watching the lights go on in the eyes of her students when they learned something new.

Vicki grew up singing in the choir at Lordship Community Church in Stratford, Connecticut, where, according to the *Hartford Courant,* her pastor, Meg Williams, recalled Soto as being full of energy and always having a bright smile. When a gunman entered her first-grade classroom at Sandy Hook Elementary School on December 14, 2012, that smile left her face forever. It was on that day that Soto taught her final and most powerful lesson. In a tribute to her, the newspaper described her actions in painful but enlightening detail.

"She ushered special education teacher Anne Marie Murphy and several children under her desk," wrote reporter Josh Kovner. "She moved other children behind a bookcase or barrier. When Lanza [the killer] came in, Soto was the only one he saw. She faced him. He killed her, and then he killed the children and Murphy under the desk. Murphy died shielding children in her arms. Other children escaped the classroom. Soto's actions saved children's lives. Only God knows what guided her."

God knows, for sure. But don't we sort of know, too? Some instinct that was housed deep inside her is what guided her—some value or trait she must have learned from the way she was raised or had seen in the people she most admired. She listened not to the voices of internal terror that would certainly come when an unstable, angry young man is pointing an already hot, overused barrel at your head, but the divine seed that resides somewhere deep in all of us and competes with fear for its rightful place at center stage.

It's no secret, really. Something in her core guided Vickie Soto on that terrible day. And because it did, a horrific massacre was made just a little less horrific for the families of the children who escaped that classroom as she made the fatal, life-giving decision to turn her body into a human shield.

I've already suggested evidences of a truly substantial spirituality. Here I add yet another. It's been known by many names: stomach, nerve, boldness, guts, backbone, valor, and perhaps at Sandy Hook Elementary simply as "What Vicki and Ann Marie had." I refer to it by its most classic and common name: courage.

Courage has been discussed with almost as many definitions and emphases as there have been commentators referencing it. One of the most helpful of those commentators for me is Lewis Smedes. He speaks from a conviction that true courage is always an outcome of true love and argues that courage is not only that which can "look evil in the face and call it evil"[26] but also "the power of love in active resistance to evil."[27]

To further make his point, Smedes moves from concept to example. "Courage is the power of a blind person to seize the world around and see it in ways that the retina of the human eye can never discover. . . . Courage is the power to grasp the intense beauty and goodness of family, friends, animals, and plants,even when we are told the newly discovered cancer will cut us off from all of these in a few months. Personal courage recreates reality because it learns to see reality in ways reborn in love."[28]

Among other things, a point Smedes makes is that courage is much more than a noble value or some fleeting feeling a person has from time to time. In Smedes' presentation of it, courage is something that is measured; it is something that is seen. It's what he calls "love's power."[29] And it insists on rejecting the kinds of unhelpful things that must ultimately yield to that love.

The kind of courage that's linked to a rigorous spirituality contains the quality of knowing what to listen to and what to ignore. It's that wind in us that penetrates the cracks it finds in our doubts and, while being fully aware of them, refuses to allow them the last word. Courage isn't the absence of terror; it's the presence of love. It's not some super-cowboy lack of angst, but a supernatural immersion into the only thing that can put angst in its place. Courage is *THE WILLINGNESS TO MAKE SURE THAT FEAR NEVER DICTATES ACTIONS.*

The above line contains the definition of courage for which I argue here: *"The willingness to make sure that fear never dictates actions."* It's a definition worthy of further exploration— especially if that exploration includes an awareness of what courage definitely is *not.*

COURAGE IS NOT THE ABSENCE OF FEAR

Of whom do you think when you consider the word "courage"? When I ask that question, people usually mention figures like Rosa Parks, Amelia Earhart, William Wallace, Nelson Mandela, Mother Teresa, Winston Churchill, or Martin Luther King Jr.—certainly people who would make my own personal list. Sometimes we'll even identify actors or the characters they play—John Wayne or "Dirty Harry" may be mentioned by some of my peers, while *24's* fictitious president, David Palmer, or its star, Keifer Southerland, might come to the minds of my own adult children or their friends.

These are some of the names that jump to the top of many lists in a discussion of courage. And, for the most part, these are some of the names that *should*. What's interesting to me about many of our "courage lists," though, is our tendency to name people who seem to "fear nothing and no one." In that case, the mantra through which we vet our favorite courageous folk might be something like, "He/she has no fear, therefore he/she is courageous." It's the assumption that courage and fear are never found together.

Actually, the thought that courage has nothing to do with fear is a curious one. Consider the following example: Two people are sitting in the waiting room at a local medical clinic. Both are to have blood drawn so cholesterol levels can be checked. Person A has no fear of needles and could have this procedure as effortlessly as she could eat a scoop of ice cream. But for Person B, it's just the opposite. For some reason he can't quite understand, he lives with an intense, almost debilitating fear of both doctors and syringes. The thought of having a needle poked into his arm, followed by the inevitable "fishing" that takes place when a vein can't be located while the sounds and smells of medical procedures float through the room, conjure up in him not just fear but low-grade panic. Still, different as they are, both individuals remain seated in the waiting room and both will have the procedure done.

Question: Which patient will display the highest level of courage when rolling up a sleeve and extending a bare, upturned elbow to the phlebotomist? Isn't it pretty clear that no courage is required where no fear exists? And is it not obvious that, though a modest example when compared with some of the trauma and drama some people deal with every day, for the person who has a great fear of clinical environments, and especially needles, some level of courage is required to even show up for the bloodletting in the first place?

My point is this: Not only is it not true that courage is the absence of fear, but in fact, we can never actually experience true courage apart from the *presence* of fear. In other words, for "courage" to actually be courage, a context of fear is required. Perhaps that's why Webster defines courage as "the act of facing and dealing with anything recognized as dangerous, difficult, or painful instead of withdrawing from it." Courage isn't the ability to "fear nothing;" it's the measurable conviction that fear doesn't get to call the shots.

Mark Twain wasn't the first or only person to recognize this dubious relationship between fear and courage, but he may have done the best job of communicating it. In *The Tragedy of Pudd'nhead Wilson,* he wrote, "Courage is the resistance to fear, mastery of fear, not the absence of fear."[30] I couldn't agree more. Here are a couple of examples that might help clarify this point.

In the sixth and seventh chapters of the Book of Acts, a follower of Jesus named Stephen is introduced. He is described as a man who had a good reputation among the people, was full of God's Spirit, and demonstrated exceptional wisdom. Like anyone with such impressive life credentials as those, Stephen was a sought-after person. What's disturbing about Stephen's story, though, is the fact that people didn't pursue him for his character, spiritual depth, or wisdom. No, folks—especially some of the religious leaders of his day—sought him out because of problems they had with what Stephen had come to believe about God. In short, Stephen was in hot water for his spiritual convictions and, more specifically, the fact that he actually lived them out.

Stephen was a man faced with a pretty nasty set of circumstances. He'd been seen helping and praying for people, especially those with huge physical needs. As a result, some had been miraculously healed. Not a problem? Well, perhaps not, except that Stephen had aligned himself with those who were convinced that Jesus of Nazareth had been the Jewish Messiah. In fact, he had become an excellent student and communicator of Jesus's teachings: a new and usurping kingdom with a divine agenda of hope, wholeness, justice, and the repair of broken relationships between people and God.

It wasn't as though Stephen was alone in this. In fact, even some of Jerusalem's own priests had begun to believe these same things. Nonetheless, Stephen was singled out, like that one wildebeest in a herd of thousands that happens to catch the eye of a hungry lion. Because of this, one of the great biblical examples of true courage was written.

In this case, the attack wasn't the natural result of a carnivore's need to calm her own hunger and feed her children. The personal injustice Stephen faced came about primarily because he had out-thought and outdebated those who opposed him. Stephen was attacked not in spite of, but *because* of his character and wisdom. The weapons used were misrepresentation, slander, false accusation, and ignorance.

Did Stephen display fear? The Bible never specifically mentions that he did. But displaying fear and feeling it are two different things. My guess is that he sensed the danger when he noticed his accusers grinding their teeth in anger at his every word. At the very least, he must have become aware at some point of the potential, increasingly likely, consequences of such a brilliant verbal defense of his faith. And the reader can't help but assume that at some point Stephen's chest began to tighten as he considered the false but convincing case that was being built against him.

"So they stirred up the people and the elders and the teachers of the law. They seized Stephen and brought him before the Sanhedrin. They produced false witnesses, who testified, 'This fellow never stops speaking against this holy place and against the law. For we have heard him say that this Jesus of Nazareth will destroy this place and change the customs Moses handed down to us.'"[31]

This isn't looking very promising, he must have thought. *I've said enough. Should I quit talking now and live, or should I tell these leaders the truth as I understand it—hold them accountable for what they've done—and almost certainly die?*

I'm assuming here. I admit that. But what thinking person could read this account in Acts and conclude that Stephen, a man identified as wise and discerning, was unable to read the situation and sense the madness of the antagonists around him. Feeling the heat and noting the increasing rage encircling him, Stephen had to be certain of the gruesome punishment that was coming as a result of his truth-telling.

Was Stephen afraid at any level? Count on it. You and I sure would have been. But he was courageous. He wasn't about to allow fear to dictate his actions. When fear said, "Run," Stephen stood. When fear said, "Be quiet," Stephen spoke up. When fear said, "Oh no. Look! They're surrounding you . . . and they have large stones in their hands. This could cost a lot," Stephen paid the ultimate price. And then, when fear said, "Quick, before you lose consciousness, condemn them for what they have done!" Stephen forgave instead, and then had the audacity to ask God to do the same.

That, friends, is courage: not the absence of fear but the mastery of it. It's the willingness to make sure fear never dictates actions.

"In these days of catastrophic change and calamitous uncertainty, is there any man who does not experience the depression and bewilderment of crippling fear, which like a nagging hound of hell, pursues our every footstep?"[32] My answer would be no. But if ever there was a person who might have proved me wrong, it was the man I quote in opening this paragraph, Dr. Martin Luther King Jr. Apparently even Dr.

King, unquestionably one of the greatest and most courageous leaders of modern history, had as one of his most tenacious and mystifying companions significant fear.

I love the way one preacher put it in a sermon designed to lead members of a Colorado congregation in celebration of Dr. King on the weekend our nation sets aside for that purpose.

"I wonder if Dr. King was ever afraid. There was a great deal to be afraid of. Nothing seemed to stop him; but fear could have paralyzed him, and he could have just continued on quietly as a pastor at a church or as a professor at a university. Fear could have stopped him in 1956, when the first bomb was thrown onto his porch. Fear could have stopped him in 1958, when he was stabbed in the chest. Fear could have stopped him when he was handcuffed the first, second, fourth, or eighth time. Fear could have stopped him in 1963, when four little girls were killed inside their Sunday school classroom."[33]

Note that this preacher doesn't argue that Dr. King "feared not," but seems to assume that he experienced the very fear he so often addressed. It was not a gentle fear that functioned as Dr. King's "nagging hound of hell," but one that "could have stopped him" and probably *would* have stopped most of the rest of us. His was the kind of fear that is only overcome when it's rendered irrelevant by taking steps to ensure that it won't be allowed to outshout the noblest cries of a concerned heart, an informed mind, or an oppressed people.

This fear with which even the great Dr. King wrestled was the kind that not only invited defeat but made possible true courage. It was both the killer and creator of character; the spoiler and shaper of leaders; the tempter and the prover of greatness. That he experienced fear as both poison and antidote, being convinced that it could either destroy or build, seems to be clearly reflected in his writings. "Normal fear protects us; abnormal fear paralyzes us. Normal fear motivates us to improve our individual and collective welfare; abnormal fear constantly poisons and distorts our inner lives. Our problem is not to be rid of fear, but rather to harness and master it."[34]

Another author said it differently, but said virtually the same thing: "'Be not afraid' does not mean we cannot have fear. Everyone has fear, and people who embrace the call to leadership often find fear abounding. Instead, the words say we do not need to *be* the fear we have. We do not have to lead from a place of fear, thereby engendering a world in which fear is multiplied."[35]

But perhaps the best example of Dr. King's sense of connection with the idea that courage and fear are actually inseparably linked came when he referred to courage as "the power of the mind to overcome fear"[36] and argued that courage was "an inner resolution to go forward in spite of obstacles and frightening situations." It was with that in mind that he challenged his listeners to "build dykes of courage to hold back the flood of fear."[37]

During some recent extended airplane travel, I watched the HBO miniseries "Band of Brothers." It's based on the true story of "Easy Company" and their strategic but incredibly costly involvement in some of the most brutal battles of World War II. Though riveting and excellently presented, it wasn't the filmed re-enactments that stood out to me most. Instead, I was captivated by the interviews with the actual men whose stories were being told. I didn't count them, but in those interviews I'm certain there were more allusions to two topics than to any others: "fear" (and/or "being afraid") and "courage" (or "heroic actions"). It's no surprise to me that these two words were so often mentioned together when those men spoke, because the footprints of courage are always preceded by the enticements of fear.

Fear is not the antithesis of courage; it's the opportunity for it, the soil around it, the birthplace of it. No, courage is not the absence of fear, it's the right response to it.

COURAGE IS NOT THE SAME THING AS RECKLESSNESS

In his instructions for the way pastors should conduct themselves in their dealings with people, Thomas Oden lifts up the need for courage. But he is also quick to caution against allowing the presence of courage to turn into what he refers to as "the vice of foolhardiness."[38] His point is not unlike that of Gregory of Nyssa who, in discussing what he implied was "the virtue of courage," argued that while cowardice is the lack of it, "rashness is its excess."[39] In trying to understand courage by noting some of what it is not, it's important to emphasize the insights that both modern and ancient theologians attempt to bring through their writing.

Unfortunately, I have plenty of personal experience with the confusion between courage and foolish recklessness. Here are just two painful examples from my own high school years of recklessness presenting as "courage."

It was a Saturday night and my best friend and I were in my car on our way to a dance. It was going to be a fun night of music, dancing, buddies, and hopefully a good turnout of girls from Mother Butler, Saint Lawrence, or any of the handful of local Catholic high schools for girls. We were dressed for success and primed by expectations we both knew would not be realized—at least not while we were still seniors at Archbishop Mitty High School. But hey, it was Saturday night and we were young— two of the primary ingredients for the adolescent amnesia that widens a young man's eyes and fuels his hopeless optimism. We owned the world, especially on weekends, and with "Tower of Power" blaring on the eight-track, I changed lanes to turn off of Moorpark Avenue toward our campus and the fun we had planned for that evening.

"Grec! Grec!" It was my friend Bill from the passenger's seat. He was waving his hands wildly, as though trying to shoo a nagging hornet and screaming. "Go! Go!"

"Why? What's wrong?" I asked too calmly for his liking.

"Just go. And go fast! We have to get out of here right now!"

It didn't take long for me to realize why I was getting the order for immediate ignition and liftoff. A '54 Chevy, one that very clearly was no longer powered by its original six-cylinder engine, had bolted from the freeway onramp, screamed across two lanes of traffic, and was now in hot, angry pursuit of the two of us. I really didn't need to ask, but I did anyway, more as a statement than a question, really.

"What in the world did you do, man?"

"I didn't like the way those guys were lookin' at me."

"Yeah? So?" I asked, still not quite getting it.

"So I flipped 'em off. I think I recognized one of them. They're from Bellarmine."

I'm ashamed to say it now, but back in those days, someone looking at us in a way we "didn't like" would have been reason enough to validate my friend's gesture. But the fact that immature rudeness was warranted by foolish high school rivalry rules didn't mean those rules couldn't be ignored on the way to a dance. Somewhat frustrated that my passenger didn't also understand that, I downshifted into second and smoked my tires as I turned into our school's neighborhood.

"Are you crazy?" I yelled through a deviant smile. "There were four of 'em in there!"

My friend's smile was even wider as he responded, "Be a man! Show some courage! Besides, the two of us could take those guys."

He was wrong on several points. Fortunately we never had to test that last crazy notion. My car was faster than theirs, I had a good head start on them, and we knew the neighborhood better—including all the best hiding places. We found one, backed in, shut off the lights, ducked down in our seats, and sat for an hour. We were too busy high-fiving each other (and secretly a little too scared) to think about driving to the dance any sooner than that.

When we finally did get to the dance, we hopped the back fence, just for the thrill of being chased by the security guards, ran into the crowd of students, made our way to the main door, paid our entrance fee (we didn't want to steal from our own school, after all), then linked up with some friends to see what else the night might have in store.

We experienced a lot of things that evening, including some pretty crazy thrills. But what we did had nothing to do with courage. Recklessness, yes. Courage, no.

Even though we didn't grow up in a small town, our high school years were among those that, by today's standards, would be considered amazingly strict in some ways but amazing lax in others. Cutting a class (yes, it actually mattered back then) would get you a lecture and some work to do around the campus. Shoplift and the storeowner was probably going to sit you down and chew you out in person, then make you sweep his floors or wash his windows. Get caught speeding or doing something equally illegal or stupid, and the police officer was as likely to take you home and have a three-way discussion with you and your dad as he was to write you a ticket.

These were the days when, even in suburbs like the one I grew up in, principals, shop owners, and police officers most likely knew you and your family and were reluctant to clog the courts with cases involving adolescent kids who were more guilty of being shortsighted teenagers than anything likely to lead to a career in serious crime. They were also the days before America realized it couldn't trust its citizens or those visiting from other countries. Rodney King hadn't happened yet; Columbine and

Sandy Hook hadn't happened yet; Oklahoma City hadn't happened yet; and perhaps most relevant of all, 9/11 hadn't happened yet. When I was growing up, schools were safe places and no one had yet learned to see planes as potential terrorist threats. So if what you're about to read seems a bit unbelievable, perhaps that's why.

A buddy and I (yes, the same friend who was in the passenger seat of my car that night on the way to the dance) were planning to go to an upscale theater to see a new film that had been released earlier that week. It was said to be a film destined for greatness—a future classic not to be missed. Being of Italian ancestry, I was pretty excited to see it. My friend was just interested in a good movie and more than happy to go with me. One of our high school classmates worked at that particular theater and had "provided" tickets that would get us into the movie for free. Of course, we sensed no need to wait in the lines that literally wrapped around the domed structure. Surely we could figure out something more productive to do with the three hours we had before the theater doors opened.

"Let's go get a plane and fly around the movie house. We can look down and laugh at the poor stiffs who are standing in line and paying $4.50 for a movie we're going to see for free." It was my friend, a private pilot in training and member of a local flight club who was making the suggestion.

"We can't afford that," I protested. "I only have $5.00. That's just enough to buy a large Coke, a big bucket of popcorn, and a Butterfinger bar."

"Not a problem. I belong to the club and I know the combination to the box they put all the keys in. Sometimes when guys rent a plane and are leaving after hours, the club owners just leave the keys and a checkout sheet in the box. We'll just borrow one of those planes, fly it around the valley, bring it back, refuel it, charge the fuel to the club, and put the key back before anyone notices."

"Really? You're sure we won't get caught?"

"Absolutely sure," he promised.

"Too good! I'm in," I said. And off we went.

The fact that we actually did "borrow" a plane and fly it over the very movie line into which we would be cutting later that evening should be enough to illustrate the point I'm trying to make with these brief stories. Sadly, though, there's more. For as we lined up our single-engine piper on the runway and began the steady roll toward takeoff, I somehow came to the conclusion that it would be a wonderful idea if my friend, only approved for solo flights at the time and forbidden under any circumstances to take passengers up with him, would teach me to take off and fly the plane. We were rolling at about thirty miles per hour when I asked him a question. Actually, it was more of a dare.

"Let me take it off and fly it!" I yelled over the sound of the roaring engine and swirling winds. "I want to try it."

"No. It's too risky. Besides, I could get in trouble. I'm not approved for passengers yet. I'm only supposed to fly solo until I get approved. I could lose my license."

"What are you talking about?" I reasoned. "We stole the stinkin' plane! Do you really think anyone's going to care about you letting me take the wheel if we get caught? Let me fly it."

We were gaining speed pretty quickly, and liftoff was only seconds away. The window was closing so I used the only line I knew would work. "Come on, man. Show some metal. Let me fly it."

That was when the foolishness that so often passes for courage in the adolescent mind took over in both of us. "Okay. Pull back steadily in three, two, one . . ."

We circled the valley for about an hour, my friend's hands rarely touching the steering wheel and pedals. Then, after landing (fortunately neither of us was daring enough to allow me to try that), we refueled the plane (charging it to the flight club, of course), drove to the theater, cut into the front of the longstanding line, and watched Coppola's "The Godfather" from seats for which we never even paid.

Courage? Not so much. I think most of us would have other words to describe what we did that evening—words like foolishness, thoughtlessness, irresponsibility, carelessness, or even criminal activity, all of them much closer to the truth. Because most of us already know that recklessness and courage are not the same thing, not the same thing at all.

Lest it appear as though the only examples to be taken from younger adults are negative ones, let me present to you a refreshing thing: an adolescent who got courage right.

In contrast to the juvenile idiocy illustrated in the previous two stories, consider the example of a teenager from another time. David, eventually a great King of Israel, was an extraordinary young man even though, like my friend and me back in 1972, he had a tendency to make risky choices. Like us, he found it difficult to back down from a challenge. And, like us, he made a decision that put him well out of his depth.

We don't know exactly how old he was when he stood and flexed his muscles against the seasoned warrior Goliath. We only know that, like us, he was "a youth." But that's where the similarities end. For this young person was not driven to dangerous activity out of ignorance or the need to yield to the boyish insecurities that are often behind some of the crazy things young men do. His willingness to take a dare was the result of conviction and passion, not some hopeless addiction to risk. That becomes clear as we look at the details of David's famous encounter with a size 10XL behemoth as recorded in the Old Testament book of I Samuel.

You don't have to be a Bible student or even particularly religious to know about and appreciate David's trademark act of courage. How could anyone not respect it? David watches as a nine-and-a-half-foot-tall Andre the Giant of a man—a gravel-voiced, tried and tested warrior who has never known defeat—comes to the crest of a hill wearing one hundred and twenty-five pounds of armor and holding up a spear, the head of which weighs something on the order of fifteen pounds. With his armor-bearer dwarfed but standing alongside him, the giant bellows out an insulting dare to any member of the army camped on the opposing hill to come and meet him in the ravine for a one-on-one, winner-take-all battle to the death.

David is astonished as Israel's host of warriors trembles in silence, and is incensed by what he sees. Then, unwilling to contain himself anymore, David, armed with nothing more than a common slingshot and a few smooth stones, and wearing no armor at all, cautiously walks down the hill, makes short work of the enemy, then cuts off his mangled and bearded head. Instantly young David becomes the catalyst for a military rout, as that single act jolts Israel's once passive army into inspired action against their archenemies, the Philistines.

A lucky shot from a crazy kid with nothing to lose and an opportunity to make a name for himself? I'm sure some of David's countrymen thought that. In fact, the Bible makes no secret of the disgust and suspicion David's own brother had for him for coming to the front line at all. One can only imagine how his brother's contempt grew when word got out that the king had initially sent for David, had actually been talking with him about placing the outcome of the entire battle in his hands, and was about to commission him to go down to represent Israel in a fight to the finish with Goliath. The historian that wrote I Samuel, though, makes no mention of a selfish motive on David's part. Instead he's pretty clear that David's actions were simply the result of raw courage. But this was a courage driven by two things and two things only.

First: David's courage comes exclusively out of a deep conviction. He's shocked to hear that the reward being offered to the person who agrees to fight the menacing giant is so high, and expresses his disapproval pretty clearly.

"What will be done for the man who removes this reproach of Israel? The king will do *what?* There should be no need to offer

such a reward! Who is this guy that such a price should be placed on his head?"

Apparently it was David's conviction that the privilege of silencing this enemy should have been reward enough! Later, as he approaches his adversary, David's convictions leak out again when he rebukes Goliath for taunting not only the armies of Israel but the God they worship. David is too principled to stand by and listen to that any longer. The flames of true courage are always lit that way; they are always ignited by a deep sense of what's right and what's wrong—of what must be protected and what must never be tolerated. That was the case with young David. His courage was born of that kind of pure conviction.

Second: David's courage came linked to his proven abilities. That courage had been tested before, and he had gained through those trials a sense that when a person responded to what simply had to be done, good things could happen. I suspect that though he wasn't absolutely certain he *would* defeat Goliath, there was no doubt in David's mind that he *could*. Before he went down to the fight, David had a pretty interesting conversation with his king. Here it is as recorded in that famous chapter of the Bible:

"David said to Saul, 'Let no one lose heart on account of this Philistine; your servant will go and fight him.'

Saul replied, 'You are not able to go out against this Philistine and fight him; you are little more than a boy, and he has been a warrior from his youth.'

But David said to Saul, 'Your servant has been keeping his

father's sheep. When a lion or a bear came and carried off a sheep from the flock, I went after it, struck it and rescued the sheep from its mouth. When it turned on me, I seized it by its hair, struck it and killed it. Your servant has killed both the lion and the bear; this uncircumcised Philistine will be like one of them, because he has defied the armies of the living God. The Lord who rescued me from the paw of the lion and the paw of the bear will rescue me from the hand of this Philistine.'

Saul said to David, 'Go, and the Lord be with you.'"[40]

When offered an excuse to actually yield to his fears, David argues that when those fears had been tested in the past, they had proven irrelevant. He wants King Saul to know he isn't just dreaming when he says he can deliver the giant. David is convinced he actually has abilities learned in the classrooms of experience, and he plans to bring them to the task at hand. His courage was certainly not limited to what he already knew he could do, but it was obviously informed by it. This courage was linked to proven ability.

Courage must never be confused with recklessness or the need to prove something. When an apparently courageous act is pure and true, it is such because it comes as a result of firmly held convictions and loosely held abilities. It's that kind of courage—the kind that can compel a person to march toward difficult contexts of opportunity and need—that's a clear mark of a dominant spirituality. And this teenage warrior who would eventually replace Saul as king had buckets of it.

COURAGE IS NOT THE SAME AS "ENFLAMED VERBOSITY"

There is an old saying I really like. It goes like this: "One who puts on his armor should not boast like one who takes his off." Modern translation? "No trash-talking allowed." That would make for a good national law—that way people might be spared the embarrassment of talking a real courageous line only to follow up their brave words with less than spectacular efforts. Wouldn't *that* be a refreshing change?

We are a "trash-talking" society—a people who seem to have lost any sense of the difference between saying something and doing something. We have "trash talk" websites, "trash talk" mugs, "trash talk" apparel, and even "trash talk" instruction videos. We love to employ the vocabulary of the courageous victor before we've even laced up the shoes we'll wear in the contest. And as if that isn't enough, sometimes we even assume that speaking like a brave person actually *makes* us one. It's a surprisingly easy error to embrace.

Things weren't that different in David's day. When young David first walked into camp with bread for his three older brothers and cheese for their captain, he arrived with the assumption that his father was correct when he said the army was in the valley of Elah, "fighting with the Philistines." What he found, though, was something quite different. Oh, he saw the soldiers, dressed and organized for war under the command of their king and under the guidance of their captains. But where David anticipated a chance to observe the army of his people engaged in courageous physical conflict with their enemy, he observed instead little more than a boisterous enactment—antiquity's version of trash talk. It sounded big and bold, but it must have left his young and glorious heart empty and perplexed.

The only battle Saul's army was in that day was a battle of words. They had abandoned true courage for the *appearance* of it in the form of what I call "enflamed verbosity." Consider these recorded facts:

- When Goliath presented himself, the mere sight of him is said to have caused Israel and their king to be "greatly afraid." In other words, there wasn't a man in Saul's army who didn't feel his blood run cold when they saw the giant and heard him defy any one of them to meet him in combat. One text even adds that they were so afraid that they fled from Goliath, perhaps to the farthest corners of their camp, well away from the sound of his intimidating growl.

- It's made quite clear that Goliath did this twice a day (once in the morning and once in the evening) for forty consecutive days.

- Yet the text tells us that on the day David arrived in camp with the supplies from his father, he found the army "going out in battle array and shouting the war cry."

So let's put all of this together. Every day, twice a day, for forty days, the Philistine army and the Israeli army got dressed for battle. And every day, twice a day, for forty days, they formed their lines. Then, every day, twice a day, for forty days, they shouted their battle cry, as though they had some intention of actually doing something that remotely resembled what they were shouting. Then, after a hard day of verbal pseudo-battle, they would go back to their camps, sharpen their swords, check their bows, eat dinner, and rest up for the next day's brave shouting match.

Courage is not "enflamed verbosity." It has little to do with talking about what you are going to do or *would* have done. There is no sword-rattling, or taunting, or "pipe-dreaming" in courage. Courage is not standing atop a hill where fear constrains us, leaving us no option other than the pretense of boldness. It's not participation in what amounts to little more than a warriors' masquerade party. Courage is saying to those fears that seek to paralyze us, "You'll have to wait until later to tempt me," then walking, albeit with shaking knees sometimes, down the hill to an almost certain death with intent to cut out the heart of a lying foe (whether that foe is a system, a philosophy, a government, or a person) that's robbing the world of hope and, therefore, must be defeated.

Courage is had, as Ronald Rolheiser puts it, "when on the basis of something more powerful than our fears we emerge from our locked rooms and begin to take down walls."[41]

Sometimes we understand what a thing is by gaining better understanding of what it is not.

Courage is not the absence of fear. Courage is not to be confused with recklessness. Courage is not "enflamed verbosity." *COURAGE IS THE WILLINGNESS TO MAKE SURE THAT FEAR NEVER DICTATES ACTION.*

A prayer for the pseudo-fearless:

"God, I've always thought that when I had no 'peace' about moving ahead, it was You telling me to stay where I was. Now I'm thinking that, at least some of the time, that 'lack of peace' was actually little more than an abundance or fear. The next time that happens, Lord, would You lead me into and through that fear? I thought the deeply spiritual feared little of nothing. Now I know that isn't true at all. I'm not asking You to kill my fears, God. I'm asking You to kill my FEAR of my fears—even while You increase my willingness to move ahead in spite of them. Amen."

CHAPTER SIX
FAITH

*It was a challenge of faith, the ultimate question
being, "Is God up to providing for me?"*

FAITH:

The Willingness to Live with the Consequences of a Godly Choice

There was a restaurant we liked in Portland, Oregon, called "Fuddruckers." I'm ashamed to say that I sold myself just inside the main entrance there late one winter evening in 1991. Fortunately, my eldest son brought me back to my senses just in time to save me.

I loved Fuddruckers. They served beautiful, huge French fries. And not far from any of the tables in the place were artery-clogging islands of accessories where you could pump hot cheese out onto those fries. We're not talking that carcinogenic slop they try to pass off as hot cheese at major-league baseball games as they sell you what they try to pass off as nachos, mind you. This was *good* cheese—thick, slow-flowing Wisconsin gold!

And Fuddruckers had massive burgers—real "chin drippers." You could pump that good, hot Wisconsin cheddar onto those burgers too. Then, when you bit into one, something magical happened: "stuff" (the truest way to describe what funnels out the end of a good burger when properly scarfed) dribbled down your chin, across your arms, off your elbows, and onto the table. That's how it ought to be when you eat a good burger, and that's one of the reasons I loved going to Fuddruckers.

But as good as the food was, it wasn't the best reason for choosing "The Fudd" when eating out. Fuddruckers' best feature by far was the sign that hung in the front window. It read, "Kids Eat Free." I loved restaurants with signs like that when our kids were young. A restaurant could have offered well-seasoned cardboard on its menu in those days and still had my business as long as the children got to eat there gratis. The promise of free food for our children worked like restaurant catnip to me back then. Why? Because we were always broke, and, well, we had three kids.

So one mid-March evening we decided to shuttle over to Washington Square to eat dinner at one of our favorites. In less than fifteen minutes we were there, in front of the restaurant, with our kids all lined up like little ducklings ready to waddle into one of the family's local ponds. But before we went in I gathered them into a huddle. It was time to set some ground rules and get on the same page before we entered the water.

Anyone who has children knows the script. You have to instruct them in order to ensure that everyone knows the plan for ordering. Otherwise, one of them might make a move we used to call "pulling a Josh."

Most families have at least one child like our second-born—that son or daughter for whom every trip to McDonalds was another opportunity to recite the phrase, "Yes, please supersize it."

"No," you correct. "We're ordering from the kids' menu. There is no supersizing with the kids' menu."

That's when the really brilliant ones shift to their secondary strategy. Our Josh was one of those "brilliant ones." So I knew what was going on in his head. He was thinking, "Let's see . . . do I want this, this, this, or this?" Then, having been outmaneuvered on the supersize issue and unable to make a decision, his eyes would slide directly to the right-hand column of the menu and, starting at the top, trickle down the list of prices until he found the most expensive offering. Assuming that the most expensive options were also the best-tasting, he would then look back over to the left-hand column, read what was printed there, and say, "I'll have one of those." He's a fantastic son, and was definitely worth the extra cost, but back then, one kid who wandered off the straight and narrow at the ordering station could ruin the entire meal.

So there we were in front of Fuddruckers—me down on one knee like the caring parent and experienced strategist I had become, and our three children, completely unaware of the real cost of things but very anxious to be allowed to eat. "You will order off the children's menu. You know what I'm talking about, right? Say it for me: 'I will only order from the children's menu.'" They all repeated it, Josh out of a dutiful heart, but with considerably less passion than the other two. "Because this is Fuddruckers, " I continued, "and at Fuddruckers kids eat free . . . but only if they order from the children's menu. And I'm determined to do our whole 'family out' thing for about fifteen bucks tonight. Now, do you understand, guys? Are you with me? Because as soon as I'm sure we're all together on this, we can go in and eat."

Affirmatives came from all three little faces, so I gave my wife Brenda the thumbs up and said, "We're good to go, honey. It's all good now. Let's eat." Rolling her eyes, Brenda opened the door and we entered.

Immediately Josh was confronted with an intense temptation. I knew this because I saw his eyes drifting to the wrong menu and heard the pain in his voice as he chose the children's hamburger. Knowing how difficult that was for him, I felt a surge of pride. *What an excellent son!* I said to myself. Then, in classic "Josh style," he added an extra-large order of fries from the adult page. I could live with it—especially since he had (and *still* has) such a warm, enriching heart and personality.

Becca, caring more about the "New Kids on the Block" video game in the next room than which menu she was being forced to use, looked up at her eldest brother. Seeing that he wasn't yet ready to order, she spoke next. Strange, since she always preferred to go last.

"Children's hot dog, please." My admiration for her peaked. So did my hope of having dinner out as a family and coming away "whole." The only one of our children yet to order was our eldest son, and experience told me that he would be no problem.

I never had to worry about David when we ate out. He was one of those kids who never wanted to step over the line and always tried to stick to the rules, as though he could feel my pain when anyone ordered anything other than a grilled cheese sandwich or a small salad and glass of water with lemon. But this time, David paused and stepped back.

Why hadn't he ordered first? We almost always did that by birth order, and even though Josh had jumped the gun, everyone expected Becca, always our quiet one in public, to be the last to decide. What could David possibly be thinking about? And what was it that had sidetracked him there at the counter? There was no way he'd ever consider ordering off the adult menu, was there? Our firstborn was always a "children's menu" shoe-in, a "kids eat free" automatic, a parent's dream ... or so I thought. But when I asked him what he wanted, he just stood there, staring at a note that had been framed and placed by the register.

"David?" I asked. "What are you having, son?"

There was what I interpreted as a mix of confusion and angst in my son's eyes when, instead of answering, he walked over to me and, with a pained look on his face, a look that almost seemed to apologize for what he was about to say, signaled the need to whisper in my ear. Then, speaking in a hushed tone, as though we were spies and the enemy had just entered the room, he said, "Dad."

"What? Do you have a problem?"

"No, but Dad, just whisper. Don't talk out loud. I . . ."

"Just order off the children's menu and we're good to go."

"But Dad, it says."

"I don't *care* what it says!" I was speaking now in that "shout mode" that parents know how to use when they're forced by circumstance or context to whisper but haven't yet corralled the eruptions that are going off in their hearts. "Just order off the children's menu; just pick one of those things listed there. If you have to have a hot dog, then you have to have a hot dog. That's the way it is when you're a kid. Besides, Mom and Becca never finish their meals. If you want something else, you can just have the rest of theirs."

"But Dad, it says the children's menu . . . the 'kids eat free' menu . . . it's for kids twelve and under."

"Right. Twelve and under. So?"

"Dad, remember? Two weeks ago, I had a birthday. I'm thirteen now. I can't order off the children's menu anymore."

This inconvenient new little fact had to be irrelevant for that one evening, I reasoned internally. I mean, wasn't there a fudge factor for kids with recent birthdays? Twelve really meant "twelve, sort of" didn't it? Besides, I was convinced if I let David order off the adult menu, I could say goodbye to getting out of there for fifteen bucks. To cave over this minor detail would cost me at least another $7. And that was only if the other two kids never got wind of it. Let that happen, I figured, and there would almost certainly be some sort of children's menu revolt.

Most of us know there is often a considerable difference between truth and spin. And the truth was surely being spun in my head that night. The spin was that this was an economic challenge, a financial decision—a clear issue of stewardship; and I certainly wanted to be a "good steward" of our budget. Church planters, which is what I was at that time, didn't make much money, so even a simple burger out at a place like Fuddruckers had to be planned with consideration for the family budget. My head had spun this as an issue of dollars and cents, with success defined as getting the family fed for a certain cost. What I failed to see was that, though it was an issue of stewardship (the stewardship of one's heart and character), it really wasn't an issue of money.

No. What I was actually facing had little to do with finances. What was it really? It was a challenge of faith, the ultimate question being, "Is God up to providing for me?" When I'm in a situation where being honest costs me a few more dollars, is my faith substantial enough to believe God is able to make up for the extra charge? If I do the right thing, will He kick it in gear and make sure I'm covered, or is $7 going to sound His alarms, sending error messages across every ATM screen in Heaven because the creator of the Earth and all that roams it has tried to make a withdrawal only to find that He has run out of money?

Looking back, I admit it was a pretty ridiculous "head discussion." But there I was, considering an opportunity to barter away the practicalities of my faith for what amounted to pocket change.

I was a Christian, a pastor, and more importantly, a dad—a molder of young men and women. But right there, in front of the order counter at Fuddruckers, with my wife looking on and a line forming behind us, I voluntarily walked up imaginary gallows stairs, stepped onto the trapdoor, and placed the noose around my own neck. Because, looking into the eyes of a tenderhearted, well-intentioned son, my response to his honest dilemma was, "Yeah? Well tonight you're twelve."

His response was an unintentional yet startling slap.

"That's not honest, Dad. And the regular hamburger is only seven dollars. What if I help you pay? I still have some of my birthday money."

WHAM!! Just like that my heart was in a clamp. My nose was feeling fuzzy. I had to excuse myself and go outside to clear my head. It was as though God was pointing at me and talking with the angels in Heaven saying, "Get a load of that pastor of Mine there in Oregon. All this week he's been asking Me to give him the kind of faith it takes to live the life I dream of for him, and tonight he can't even round up enough trust in Me to cover a seven-dollar upcharge!"

I was only outside for a couple of minutes, but my family probably felt I was gone longer than that. When I finally came back in, I walked straight over to David.

"Forgive me, Scudder. You're right. Go ahead and order off the adult menu." I dared not even glance over at eleven-year-old Josh, since I was certain he had already calculated the hours until is thirteenth birthday. I neither wanted nor needed to enter into renegotiations with him just then. All my focus was where it needed to be. It was exclusively on the confused son who had heard his dad preach about faith that Sunday morning, then watched him vanquish the very idea of it within hours of closing the doors to the church.

That was when something powerful happened. It was the simplicity of it that was so lovely. Josh suggested we just go up to the counter and tell the truth. Perhaps they would allow David to order off the children's menu this one last time. It was such a creative initiative that I figured we might as well give it a shot. Since it was his burger that was at risk, it was David who acted on the idea.

"Sir," David reported, "I just had my thirteenth birthday a few days ago, and we came here 'cause the kids get to eat free. We didn't know there was an age limit of twelve years old. Would it be okay if I ordered one of the free meals even though I'm thirteen now? If that's not okay, I'll just have the regular hamburger and a water, please."

The young man behind the counter seemed baffled. But it didn't take long for him to realize what was happening and gather himself for a response. He looked down at our son, smiled and said, "Thank you for your honesty. Absolutely. Go ahead and order from either menu. Oh, and happy birthday."

There's an old saying that cynics love to offer. It goes something like this: *Integrity does not put bread on the table.* But on that night, the cynics lost a round—at least in the eyes of my children. Each one of them walked right past me, carrying overfull trays to the condiment table where limitless quantities of relish, mustard, catsup, and, of course, hot cheese waited to be added to complimentary dinners. I just stood and watched them, each free meal reminding me of how thoroughly I had been defeated by a "faith" so feeble it was subdued by the mere possibility of having to pay for an additional sandwich, belief in a God who was apparently incapable of working out the finances for even the easiest of challenges, and a cohort of children who fortunately hadn't yet "learned" any of those doubts that seem to be reserved for Christian adults.

My dad once told me, considerable passion mingled with disgust in this voice, "They ought to round up all you preachers and tattoo a big sign across your foreheads. It should read, 'NOT FOR SALE.''Cause when you sell yourselves to whatever pressures you all deal with, you sell out those of us who are looking to you for strength."

No need to round me up and print anything on my head that night. I had already written "SOLD" there myself. Fortunately, my own kids bought me back.

All of us have our "Fuddruckers moments"—times when, facing untenable decisions, we say to ourselves, "I know what the right thing to do is—or at least I *probably* know. But if I do it, the potential consequences could be very costly, even devastating. If I do it, I'm going to be stuck in a nasty swamp of options, and I don't really think I want to bathe there."

Martin Luther was one who knew the bumps, bruises, and costly scars of choosing to "live by faith" in those critical moments. Yet he, in giving voice to God to make his obvious point, wrote, "Will you transgress My commandment with its sure promise of blessedness on account of the uncertain possibility of future misfortune? Or will you do evil [Luther's word for anything that is wrong] in the hope that good will come of it?"[42] He was saying then what one popular band communicated in one of their hit songs: "Sometimes the hardest thing and the right thing are the same."[43]

Ultimately, faith comes down to believing that when God promises something, it's going to happen, even when—*especially* when—what He promised can't be seen or seems to be far from our grasp. The Bible, in Hebrews 11:1, puts it this way: "Faith is being sure of what we hope for and certain of what we do not see." What many call "the classic biblical definition of faith," however, may be more like a description of it. And the context of that often-used "definition" hints at there being a little more to faith than simply a one-dimensional sense of "believing" in something.

For instance, immediately before that classic "definition" is presented, verses 10:32-40 reference an obvious connection between decisions based in faith and some painful outcomes of those decisions. See especially 10:32, where the writer of Hebrews reminds his readers that, at least for them, one of the partners of spiritual clarity is significant suffering. Verses 33 and 34 even go so far as to specify some of the torment, noting that the rewards of living Christianly often include things like public ridicule and the unjust and unprovoked confiscation of personal property. Then, after the definition of faith is presented in the first verse of chapter 11, the writer lists no fewer than eighteen individuals and the entire fellowship of the prophets, connecting them and their faith with some of its even more drastic "consequences." Here's what the text says regarding some of the costs associated with their decisions to practice faith:

"And what more shall I say? I do not have time to tell about Gideon, Barak, Samson, Jephthah, David, Samuel and the prophets, who through faith conquered kingdoms, administered justice, and gained what was promised; who shut the mouth of lions, quenched the fury of the flames, and escaped the edge of the sword; whose weakness was turned to strength; and who became powerful in battle and routed foreign armies. Women received back their dead, raised to life again. Others were tortured and refused to be released, so that they might gain a better resurrection. Some faced jeers and flogging, while still

*others were chained and put in prison. They were stoned; they were
sawed in two; they were put to death by the sword. They went about
in sheepskins and goatskins, destitute, persecuted and mistreated—
the world was not worthy of them. They wandered in deserts and
mountains, and in caves and holes in the ground. They were all
commended for their faith, yet none of them received what had been
promised because God had planned something better for us so that
only together with us would they be made perfect."*

Faith is indeed the assurance of things hoped for, the conviction
of things not seen. But it seems it's also potentially connected
with a little more than assurance and conviction—things like
having your name dragged through the mud, your personal
possessions confiscated, imprisonment, torture, stonings, being
sawn in two while still alive, and being put to death by the sword.
And in the event one is allowed to live a public expression of
faith, that life is often one only the insane would choose:
wandering the streets while destitute and hungry and wearing
what amounts to rags. Tough consequences, to say the least.

In his excellent book, *Missional Church,* Darrel Gudar writes
that this thing we call faith "means taking the risk that acting
like Jesus may bring the same fate it brought Jesus. It means
being willing to trust Jesus's way, all the way—rather than
resorting to some other way . . . in an effort to prevent ill
consequences or to protect one's own life."[44]

Is faith about assurance and conviction, as Hebrews 11 reports?
Yes, but not in a way that guarantees some sort of lollipop ending
or outcome. Apparently, the practice of "Hebrews 11 faith" is
connected to the presence of difficulty—very *significant* difficulty!
At least that's what the writer of the epistle seems to be saying.
It's with this in mind that I suggest a definition of faith that

is pragmatic and measurable. It too is probably more of a description than a definition. Nonetheless, here it is again: *FAITH IS THE WILLINGNESS TO LIVE WITH THE CONSEQUENCES OF A GODLY CHOICE.* It's living with the conviction that only a weak-thinking fool would expect healthy results from infected choices. It's being measurably surrendered to the fact that when it comes right down to it, honor feels better and has a better ending than any of the many things for which it is often exchanged. It's believing not only the assertions of John 3:16, but those of Romans 8:28 as well. It is remembering that faith, at least insofar as it speaks to the issue of Christian spirituality, addresses not only a person's "source of life" but his or her "way of life" too. It's having the audacity to believe that when telling the truth about your son's age costs you an additional $7 at dinner, God is able to either cover the tab or lead you to a place where you don't mind covering it yourself.

By this definition, *"the willingness to live with the consequences of a Godly choice,"* faith works a lot like the old software program I used in the early days of personal computers. I always wanted to have my expanded sermon notes fit on both sides of an 8 ½ x 11 sheet of typing paper; that way I could easily file them, yet still have enough space to write down all I would need if I wanted to refer to a particular sermon for later use. And though I never liked the idea of preaching from a full manuscript, an expanded outline allowed me all the help I might need were I to forget exactly how I wanted to state a delicate or particularly important point.

Occasionally—who am I fooling?—*often,* I would find I had much more sermon information than I could fit on two sides of a page. To fix that, I had to go to the top of the completed document and set new margins. In that old program I would punch a series of buttons to reveal the old margin codes. Then, going to the margin settings for the top of the page I would type in zero. I'd repeat those same steps for both the bottom and side margins. The next step was my favorite part. It was fun to sit back and just watch it happen. I would hit the F-10 key and watch as the new margins would just trickle down the screen, repositioning sentences in such a way that two and a half pages of typed text was forced to fit onto two sides of only one sheet of paper. The margins were narrow, but everything always stayed on the page. In other words, none of the words ever fell off onto the floor.

That's sort of how this definition of faith works. Sometimes making decisions that are honorable and right results in a life that feels as though it's being squeezed right off the sheet. Faith does what's right anyway and trusts God with the task of repagination. It harbors a conviction that, even when telling the truth may mean no one wants to buy the car you're selling; even when practicing financial generosity means it may be a little more challenging to make the budget work that month; even when you refuse to do unethical things just so you might land that new client and keep your job, whatever happens as a result will work out for good. Faith believes that in those circumstances, God will be able to rearrange life's document in such a way that all the text will still fit on the page.

When we finally become willing to quit rewriting and redefining things, we realize that most of the decisions we're responsible to make are not difficult to figure out. If we're honest, we usually already know exactly what we should do. The hard part is deciding to pull the trigger once we know it. Granted, there are seasons when a lack of clarity will arise, when we must knock a little harder or call a little more often to get an answer—they just don't occur nearly as often as we might like to pretend.

In short, the majority of our tough choices are little more than "Fuddruckers moments," where we already know what should happen—where the right thing is already fairly obvious. What's sometimes *not* so obvious is whether or not we've got the stomach, the "faith" to do what *ought* to be done.

Let's face a painful truth about faith: Too often, the only real difference between what we call "tough decisions" and what seem to be easy ones is the "price tag" or magnitude of the consequences. Faith keeps pointing to that inconvenient fact, then daring us to choose based on a thing's inherent rightness instead of its potential outcomes. It's in that sense that *faith is the willingness to live with the consequences of a Godly choice.*

That's all well and good. But unless there is evidence of it being practiced in scripture, this definition of faith is little more than an exercise in semantics. Fortunately, the Bible is *full* of people who seem to have been living with this working understanding of faith. I'll dive into but two of the many examples.

In an Old Testament search for the employment of this kind of faith, I could cite any of a number of people. Ruth certainly had a few consequences to consider before she did what she knew God wanted her to do. Moses may be one of the strongest arguments for faith as the willingness to live with the consequences of a Godly choice, along with Gideon and his army, Deborah and all the challenges of being Israel's first female leader, and Abraham as he reluctantly sharpened the knife he would use to slit the throat of his own son and offer him as a human sacrifice. But the person we will observe, for no reason other than that his is such an unconventional yet clear example, is Isaiah in Isaiah chapter 6.

Isaiah's vision as recorded in that bewildering chapter is certainly spectacular, if not frightening. It's a text so well-rehearsed in some religious communities and so accurately quoted in some nonreligious settings that it almost needs no explanation. But for the sake of the point, I'll summarize it here.

Isaiah 6 records him having a vision where he walks through a door and into a forbidden room. The description of that room is dazzling. The context is otherworldly and way beyond normal human experience. The first thing the prophet notices are heavenly beings in the process of worshipping God. He's never seen anything like them before. Then, as though that weren't enough to stop his heart, Isaiah's vision suddenly has him gazing upon God himself.

God is described as lofty and exalted—the center of all attention as he sits upon his throne. His robe takes up almost all space in the temple, barely leaving room for a few furnishings and the strange-looking, wing-flapping worshippers hovering around him. It's certainly not a silent vision. Those worshipping, floating creatures are singing in a language Isaiah doesn't know but, for some reason, can understand: "Holy, Holy, Holy, Holy. The fullness of the earth is this one's glory." Then, as though there hasn't already been enough to leave an appropriate impression, the place starts to shake while white smoke materializes out of thin air.

I've always loved Isaiah's words, the response like that of a little child who just realized he had poked his head into a place where it definitely didn't belong. In effect he says, "Uh oh. I'm dead meat. I don't measure up to any of this. All I see when I look at myself from this perspective is filth. I'm vastly inferior. Even the loftiest words that come out of my mouth are dust, and the people to whom I speak those words—even on their best days—appear as refuse. I wouldn't have said that a few minutes ago. But now that I've seen this . . . and especially *Him*, I'll never be able to understand things any other way."

Did I take a few liberties with that paraphrase? Of course. But you get the sense of what was happening as Isaiah declares, "Woe is me, for I am a man of unclean lips, and I live among a people of unclean lips."

The next thing that happens has to be startling if not downright terrifying for Isaiah. One of the seraphim that had been previously occupied with worship sees him peeking in on what human eyes should normally never see. Having noticed him, it flies over to where Isaiah is standing. But that isn't the most alarming part. The scariest part, as I try to imagine what Isaiah might have been thinking, is what that being was bringing with it. In its hand, Isaiah reports, the creature was carrying something it had removed from God's altar. It was a coal so white-hot that it had to be carried with tongs. Isaiah must have assumed, given his new perspective of himself and his people, that he was going to get from that seraphim exactly what he was now convinced he deserved—death by fire.

I wonder if the prophet didn't duck or clench his fist and screw up his face as he felt the heat of the coal near his mouth and anticipated the burning pain. Then, just before his lungs took what he assumed would be their last tortured breath, he was surprised. Instead of the death he was certain he had earned, Isaiah received mercy. The coal from the altar of God was used not to destroy him but to purify him. He experienced not judgment but forgiveness, compassion.

The next verse is almost comical when you think about it. God offers a question: "Whom shall I send? Do you have any ideas about who should go for us?"

Looking over both of his shoulders and noticing that no one else had entered the room, Isaiah responded, "Here am I, Lord" (and I *am* alone here, right?). "Send me."

Accepting an assignment from God before you even know what that assignment entails is enough to make my point. For that demonstrates tremendous faith, displaying a certain willingness to live with the consequences of a Godly choice. But in my mind, Isaiah showed greater faith by not taking back his words once he did know what God had in mind. For it turned out that in order for Isaiah to be successful in God's eyes, he would have to be willing to look like a complete failure in everyone else's. His call? Go and preach to people who will never be transformed, never hear and respond, never "get it."

"Go and make the heart of this people calloused," God had ordered. "Make their ears dull and close their eyes. Otherwise, they might see with their eyes, hear with their ears, understand with their hearts and turn and be healed."

Isaiah understood exactly what was being asked of him. His assignment was, in effect, to go forth and fail miserably. God was ordering him to preach in such a way that people would stay distant and mentally dim lest they return to God and find the healing Isaiah himself had just experienced.

Then things got even worse. When he inquired as to how long he would have to endure such discouragement, Isaiah found no great emotional boost. God's response must have sent that faithful servant to a place where he almost wished he had been consumed by that hot coal instead of purified by it.

"Until the cities lie ruined and without inhabitant, until the houses are left deserted and the field ruined and ravaged, until the Lord has sent everyone far away, and the land is utterly forsaken."

Great! I can't wait. Sign me up. Every prophet dreams of having a leadership task like that, right? Wrong. Few of us would accept such a call because relatively few of us have that kind of faith. Thank God Isaiah did. For he becomes one of the premier examples of the kind of faith that's linked to a mature spirituality—*the willingness to live with the consequences,* and they were significant in his case, *of a Godly choice.*

Just as there are several Old Testament examples of this definition of faith being lived out, there are also many in the New Testament. However, the ultimate example is Jesus himself in Matthew 26. That's the account of those difficult hours he spent praying in the garden just before his arrest and crucifixion.

Several things are obvious in that text. The first is something too often discounted in Jesus. It is the fact that, while praying in the garden that night, he was as strung out as any person had ever been. In other words, he was human—*fully* human. And that humanity has left its footprints all over the text in question, primarily in the emphasis on Christ's emotional state that evening.

Earlier in the chapter, Jesus predicts that he's going to be betrayed and killed. He even has his body "anointed/prepared for burial" right in the middle of a good meal at the house of Simon the leper. Imagine the comforting force of someone coming up to you this evening between bites of linguini and white clam sauce and measuring you for the coffin that will frame your corpse in the next couple of days. Then you might be getting close to understanding Christ's emotional state in those days leading up to his garden experience.

As recorded in Matthew's account, Jesus sat down to the well-known "last supper" with his disciples and announced that one with whom they had just dined would actually sell him out to the very authorities against whom they had been struggling for so long. We don't really know all that was said or thought at that dinner table. John's account, however, goes out of the way to point out that Jesus was deeply troubled in his spirit (John 13:21) as he revealed what was in store. Some Bible experts are even convinced that Jesus was actually trying to give his betrayer every chance to reconsider what he was about to do. Clearly, Jesus was a man who, though not caving to it, was feeling the strain of Judas's plans.

What human wouldn't have been disturbed by such betrayal? What was the Lord feeling as he washed Judas's feet earlier that evening? What were his eyes communicating later on as he dipped a morsel into a cup and fed it to the "friend" who would later hand him over to the authorities? How far did Christ's heart sink when his failed disciple ate the wine-soaked bread without any sign of remorse, already having looked straight into those ever-kind eyes and said with a mouth full of communion bread and wine, "Well, of course, you are certain it isn't *me* who will betray you, aren't you, my excellent teacher?" Was it at that moment that Jesus quit trying, knowing at that point, as John points out, that Judas had already surrendered himself fully to Satan? Is that why he finally resigned himself to inviting his beloved traitor/friend to go ahead and quickly do what he felt he had to do? How broken would *any* human heart be on an evening like *that* evening?

Christianity presents Jesus as fully divine. According to the Nicean Creed, he is "very God." Of that there is no question. But that same creed also points out that Jesus was fully human. To tamper with his humanity, then, or even to minimize it is to violate an orthodox Christian view of him and even call into question the purpose of his entire redemptive career. As a fully human individual, Jesus certainly knew the numbness of a lover scorned, of a loyal friend rejected. Judas had, for whatever reason, chosen a different spouse. Jesus had been dumped for someone or something else. Can it really be doubted that he would feel the full emotional force of that rejection?

The level of his inner turmoil is even more clearly seen in what happens later in the garden. Jesus carried significant emotional weight with him to that place of prayer. First and foremost was the pain that must have resulted from Judas's cold rejection of his gracious offer. Even though he warned that all of them would stumble in their faith that night, Peter had been singled out as one who would deny Jesus three times before morning, making him, at least in the eyes of some of the other disciples, the prime suspect in the plot to kill their master. Christ must have felt for Peter. Perhaps, and of course this is conjecture, that's one of the reasons he invited Peter to come along as part of the small, exclusive group that was to join him for prayer. Jesus was a leader who was, as we say, sweating bullets—not so much out of fear (even though he would have been allowed the privilege of fear as a fully human person) as out of internal heaviness.

What happens next makes the level of his inner turbulence even more obvious. Though he had three close friends with him for support, verse 37 of Matthew's account describes Jesus as being "grieved and distressed." As though Matthew wanted to drive home this point, he quotes Jesus in the next verse as saying to Peter and the two Zebedee sons, "My soul is deeply grieved, to the point of death; remain here and keep watch with me." It's as though he's saying, "Hey, man, I really need you guys right now. Watch my back. Keep me solvent. I've been giving and giving to you all this time. Now I need *you* to give to *me*. Stay with me now. Be with me like you've never been with me before." Then he went just beyond them (about a stone's throw according to Luke) and prayed.

The description of that prayer is important in grasping the emotional state of Christ. He's not described as one who simply strolled over to the nearest fallen tree, then gently knelt down for a prefabricated, formal prayer. Matthew tells us that he "fell on his face and prayed"—not "to his knees" did Jesus fall, but "*on his face.*" One can hardly read this without hearing the flop of his body and seeing the flying dust as it hovers around his beard. Tears and sweat mingled with the elements to form a holy, muddy sludge in that place as he fell. And if body language offers any clue to the volume and intensity of the actual prayer, his points to a petition of deep, audible moanings, of impassioned tones as Jesus asks of his father what he had earlier implied he would never need ask.

Further revealing the force of his internal flare-up, he makes what many would consider a shocking request: "Let this cup pass from me, please. Is there no other way?" Then, as though he hadn't already been through enough, he comes back to his already weary entourage only to find them so exhausted from their sorrow that they have fallen asleep. This not being the first time they had dozed off that night, Jesus is anything but patient with his comrades. As before, he awakens and challenges them. But this time his criticism, though loving, is harsh.

"Can't you stay awake at such a critical hour? You simply must stay alert and keep a lookout."

Things only slide downhill from there. Jesus appears to be no closer to peace. His breath is still short as he returns to his prayer spot and checks in with his father once again. Nothing new is said; Jesus repeats the same prayer, and he hears the same answer to it. Then, as though scripted, when he seeks the encouragement he so badly needs from his friends, he again finds them snoozing. This time he lets them sleep and returns to his prayerful redundancy, requesting again of his father that he be kept from the terrible experience awaiting him just around salvific history's corner.

So complete is Christ's anguish that at one point, writes Luke, an angel is dispatched to care for him as he begins to literally sweat drops of blood. Put simply, Jesus was experiencing a major emotional quake. He was clear about what the Father wanted him to do. He knew that following through with the plan The Trinity had crafted would mean personal pain and brokenness beyond any vocabulary's pathetic attempt to describe it. And he certainly knew he had a decision to make.

I wonder if, somewhere between his final "amen" and the stirring of the lapsed intercessors he loved so fully, Jesus didn't stand over his disciples and contemplate his decision the way a mother gazes upon rosy-cheeked infants slumbering in their cribs after a hard day of skinned knees and ruffled brows. Did he gently stroke their faces as he admitted that their only hope for a good future was his willingness to finish what he had started? Did he consider the sacrifices of the selfless man who raised him—a dad history would all but forget? Was he privy to the pain his mother felt every time someone stared and whispered because her swollen midsection made obvious the fact that she had become pregnant before she had been married, but not so obvious at all that the pregnancy was the result of her having been innocently chosen to carry the bastard child who would make every human life worth living again? Did he feel the same inner conflict all leaders feel while, with an eye toward their destruction, crosses are being fashioned and swords sharpened by the very ones they are trying to lead? Did God the Father whisper to God the Son that night what He has been whispering to sons and daughters ever since . . . "You have a choice to make, My child. Choose to endure whatever comes of saying yes to Me and My plot. Choose to live with the consequences of a noble, a Godly choice"?

No one knows, really. But we do know that Jesus made a determination. Faced, and not for the first time, with the opportunity to throw his lot in with what was easier, and being well aware of the human example he was for every man and woman who would pattern their lives after his between that moment and the moment he returned to Earth to make all things right again, Jesus chose the option every truly great and faithful leader chooses. He chose faith—he decided to be willing to live with the painful, bloody consequences of a thorny, lacerated, fatal, Godly choice.

"That's fine for Isaiah," you say. "He had great visions to counter his weaknesses. The ground moved for him. He heard the actual voice of God. Of course he could stay faithful in an assignment that produced no perceived gains. Every time he was tempted to sell out, all Isaiah had to do was return to the mental tapes of his famous vision of a smoked-filled room. And Isaiah had the privilege of playing those tapes whenever he needed them. Every time he licked the dry and burning lips that preached to closed ears he must have remembered the coal that had touched them, finding in those memories the fiber to keep going.

"I have no visions, no wounds of such a grace, and certainly no memory of a quaking voice that came from the throne of God.

"And Jesus? I love him and I owe him everything. But he was *GOD*, for goodness sake! When *he* struggled, angels massaged his neck. I've never walked on water, or felt healing power leave me as I held the hand of a dying friend in hospice care. I've never cursed a fig tree much less seen it die before my eyes as a result. And I can't even raise my 401k from the dead, much less my neighbors or friends.

"Sure Jesus was faithful. His prayers were symphonies where Heaven responded to every note. Mine are soliloquies. I guess I believe God listens when I pray, but sometimes it seems as though the only voice of encouragement I receive from Him when the wolves of compromise are lined up outside my tent is the one I myself imagine. Where do *I* go after I pray *my* garden prayers? What inspiration is there for *me* when I'm tempted to choose anything and everything but faith?"

I know that my options are limited only by the number of faith stories in scripture. But even though there are so many to choose from, I usually knock on the door of the same literary friend. In those traumatic moments when faith feels like my worst option, I usually find my way to Psalm 46. It almost seems it was written just for people who are wandering somewhere between a "last supper" and a "last breath." Starting with verse one, which for me is often all that needs be read, the psalm works its way to an overwhelming climax, where the limp sails of human resolve find their wind.

God is our refuge. Go and hide there when faith guarantees suffering.
God is our refuge. Take your fear there when obedience ushers in pain.

God is our refuge. Go and rest there when principled decisions invite mountains to crumble around you and tumultuous waters to crash down upon you.

God is our refuge. Run there to Him to be reminded that the city in which you now live will not be the city in which you *always* live . . . that things will not always be as they now are for you.

God is our refuge. Crawl if you must, but get to that place where with a word He keeps life from falling off the pages of the narrow margins created by the consequences of an honorable choice.

God is our refuge. Get there and review the faith tapes of Mary and Ignatius and Martin Luther King Jr.—of your grandmother or your spouse or that friend who never gave up on you. See God's works. Find strength in God's works. *Be* God's works.

God is our refuge. Find your way to that refuge. Rest in calm peace there while lightning strikes around you.

God is our refuge. Not just *any* god. Mother Teresa's God, Martin Luther's God, Mary Magdalene's God.

Collapsed lungs can breathe again when God speaks like that. At least these collapsed lungs can. I go there, to Psalm 46, when faith asks me to be more than I am. And when I get there, an otherwise silent deity usually speaks words with which he is completely familiar, offering encouragement well-rehearsed throughout history.

"Choose faith," he says. "Choose the willingness to live with the consequences of a Godly choice." And having been there with that text, sometimes—just sometimes—I actually do.

We were both sitting outside in the sun reading. In my lap was a book about management. In hers was Francis Chan's *Crazy Love*. Needless to say, Brenda was enjoying her book much more than I was enjoying mine.

"Honey, listen to this," she interrupted. I assumed that, as had been the case with her ten previous interruptions, this was going to be about me sharing in her literary discovery more than me enjoying one of my own. Wrong. This time we would *both* be stunned by what my wife was sharing. Though we had both read it already, what Chan had written stunned us as though we had never heard it before. "God doesn't call us to be comfortable. He calls us to trust Him so completely that we are unafraid to put ourselves in situations where we will be in trouble if He doesn't come through ..."[46]

We just sat there and stared at each other. To add words to what we had just heard would have only tainted it. We both knew that, though it had come through a book and from the pen of a man, we had received a message from God just then: We needed to live differently. We needed to throw some dry wood on the fires of our faith.

We needed to be more willing to live with the consequences of Godly choices. True and deepening spirituality, we reasoned, demanded it; true and deepening hearts, we were convinced, longed for it; true and deepening people, we reluctantly admitted, *did* it—they acted, then trusted. In fact, they acted in such a way that they *had* to trust.

They lived with faith.

A prayer for those with feeble faith:

"I'm thinking that some things I cherish need to be euthanized, God. I cherished financial stability but now wonder if I haven't placed more value on it than I have on investing in Your agenda. I've been convinced that You wanted to keep Your children safe and far from pain. Now I'm thinking that You value obedience and daring more highly than safety. In fact, reading about how You stood and watched as many of Your most faithful champions cried out in pain rather than deny their allegiance to You is unsettling. What are You willing to watch me struggle with? How loudly would I have to scream before You stepped in to stop my pain? I'm cautious, Lord. But I want to be found faithful. So please do one of two things: either redefine 'faithfulness' or redefine me. Amen."

CHAPTER SEVEN
YIELDEDNESS

Yieldedness is something only the most confident, secure, mature, and strong among us can actually pull off.

YIELDEDNESS:
The Willingness to Allow God to Dictate Your Personal Agenda

I took a trip to the music store recently (yes, those actually do still exist) to redeem a gift certificate I had received from a friend. It was a nice music store, the kind that almost transports you to a different world as you enter—a world that seems to know of and need nothing but lyric and tune. Entering was a little like stepping through the main gate of a Disney property. For a little while my life felt as though it had no significant challenges and all the world's problems could be solved if humanity would just listen to the right songs.

Having been greeted by row after row of CDs from every musical genre imaginable, I became aware that I was being serenaded with background music that served as an enticing melodic aroma. It was a great song that was playing, a numbingly inspiring one. So, while flipping through the CDs, and without even realizing I was doing it, I started singing along—not quite at "shower level," but well beyond a volume that's appropriate for a public store.

"Isn't that a powerful song?" It was the voice of a customer on the other side of the rack.

"Yes." I like making conversation with people I don't know so I added an opinion, "One of the greats. Right up there with Billy Joel's 'Piano Man,' Neil Diamond's 'I Am, I Said,' and Hank Williams' 'I'm So Lonesome I Could Cry.'"

"Interesting point," he lowered the CD he had been holding at chest level and, without letting go of it, looked up at me, "especially since the one you're singing and the others you mentioned appear to represent worldviews that are polar opposites."

Great! I thought to myself. *A philosopher. This isn't going to be a quick conversation.*

I was right. It wasn't quick. But it sure was helpful. By the time we were twenty minutes into it, I had forgotten all about trying to find the *Best of Neil Young* album I had come for, choosing instead to rethink the lyrical point of the song I'd been so thoughtless enjoying. My conclusion? Except as an excellent expression of a vacant approach to life and so much of what I no longer believed, the tune I had been singing in the store that day, one of the most revealing musical contributions of its genre by one of the most gifted musicians of his generation, had been spoiled for me.

It was great music that was presented with excellence, but it had been sabotaged by a toxic message. It's that message, or rather its opposite, that's the focus of these next pages.

This is a chapter about something Americans, and I'm convinced humans in general, find very difficult to do. It's a chapter about a spiritual component that can sometimes seem to be anything *but* mighty. Yet strangely, it's a chapter about a practice that demands great strength and confidence—about strapping ourselves to the mast as we navigate the waters of life so that, like Odysseus when he heard the seductive singing of coastal sirens calling him to "Come closer, famous Odysseus— Achaea's pride and glory—moor your ship on our coast so you can hear our song!" we can resist the "honey-lipped voices" of life that promise wisdom but deliver little more than wreckage and death.

This chapter is about yieldedness, something only the most confident, secure, mature, and strong among us can actually pull off. But "pull it off" we must if we're to know a lasting and helpful spirituality, because yieldedness is our primary guard against unwittingly singing along to the kind of music that, though masterfully presented and easy on the ear, contains lying lyrics that serve ultimately to captivate, misdirect, and destroy.

YIELDEDNESS IS THE WILLINGNESS TO ALLOW GOD TO DICTATE YOUR PERSONAL AGENDA. It's what John of the Cross was thinking of when he wrote about how God dwells in different people. "He lives in some as though in His own house, commanding and ruling everything; and in others as though a stranger in a strange house, where they do not permit Him to give orders or do anything."[47]

In a chapter about powerful spirituality that is focusing on "yieldedness," some may have guessed by now which song I was singing that day at the mall. It has already been made obvious that it wasn't "Piano Man," "I'm So Lonesome I Could Cry," or "I Am, I Said," with their expressions of human angst and agonizing cries for purpose and meaning.

Initially recorded by one of America's most accomplished and beloved cantors, the song I referred to advocated a philosophy that made no room for human anguish, even denying the recognition of it in the lives of truly worthwhile people. Like those others, it's a beautiful song with a brilliant tune, and musical structure that approaches genius. But unlike them, it's more a prideful statement of sufficiency than a humble expression of need. It doesn't cry, doesn't beg, doesn't want, and certainly doesn't yield.

Presenting a lyric that stands in direct opposition to just about every major religion's primary teachings about healthy spirituality is the song "My Way" by Frank Sinatra. It's good (great, really) music that, though done extraordinarily well, represents an unfortunate message—one that endorses as "strong and good" much of what Jesus believed to be weak and unhelpful, corrosive even. Yet "My Way" expresses a spirituality so compelling for the powerful and favored of our time that even many well-intentioned Christ-followers and religious leaders have found ways to embed it in their understanding of faith. Apparently even though Jesus valued the admission of human dependence, of yieldedness, many of his followers simply don't.

For instance, note some of the obvious differences between what Jesus might call "great" and what America's anthem of self-sufficiency celebrates: 1) "My Way" is about a man claiming that at the end of life, what was most important to him was that he lived it as he chose to, presumably with little regard for anyone else or any imposed standard. 2) Of course, this fellow had a few regrets, but not many. And he was proud of the fact that no one had forced an agenda on him. He was the master and planner of his course and was in charge of his destiny. Others may need to look elsewhere for leadership, but he did what he wanted to do—nothing else. 3) When he faced something that seemed to have been exceedingly tough, no need to ask for help. He simply tightened his belt, stood tall, chewed it up, and spit it out. Nothing was too much for him. 4) This pseudo-superman admitted he had pain and loss. How did he deal with it in the end, though? He forced tears to subside and laughed in the face of the challenge. Then, for dessert, he made sure that everyone knew he was anything but shy about all his self-initiated success. 5) Finally, the quintessential man is described as one who depends upon nothing and no one but himself, always says everything he feels, is not identified with one who kneels (probably a reference to losing or surrendering in general more than kneeling in prayer, but still a negative picture of yielding in any significant way), and prefers to take the blows of life directly. Others may need the shield of mercy or crutch of assistance, but this guy would rather handle all the consequences of his decisions (whether good or bad) straight on.

This is our culture's epitome of a fully actualized human being with a superior spirituality—a spirituality of self-absorbed control, intolerance for any infringement on personal right-of-way, self-initiative, and inflexibility. It's Libertarianism baptized. Great music, but it's a terrible message—terrible, at least, according to the teachings of Jesus. In fact, this lyric almost appears to be purposefully constructed to represent the antithesis of Jesus.

Strangely, even though it sounds like it takes more grit and is more difficult, Sinatra's "way" is, in my experience, much easier to navigate than Christ's "way." It's simply more demanding and challenging to live the Jesus life—the yielded life—than to simply jump onto life's merry-go-round and let its passions and preferences take you where they will. For instance, compare the lyric of "My Way" with the lyric of Christ and decide for yourself which is more challenging.

"My Way" spirituality says that we should do whatever we want, whatever comes naturally to us, never making concessions for other people we meet. I've NEVER had a difficult time doing that. Conversely, Jesus teaches we should treat other people the way we would want to be treated ourselves. His way is the way of not only forgiving our enemies but helping them in life.[48] That has NEVER been easy. It has always taken more strength and character than I've been able to summon to consider others as more important than myself, and even admit my need for them.[49] And to help, bless, and pray for my enemies? Who *does* that? It's just too tough, even for the best of us.

"My Way" spirituality has very few regrets, takes direction from no one, and rejects the idea that there is any value in dependence. Jesus modeled a quite different standard. In fact, he was so committed to the idea of being led that even he was unwilling to set his own agenda, choosing instead to discover the preferences of his father and follow *them*.[50] In fact, Jesus went so far as to say that our dependence upon God for leadership should be so severe that we actually lose our own lives, set them aside in favor of surrendering to the life he modeled for all of humankind.[51]

Choose for yourself which is more difficult and unnatural to do. Does it take more steam to simply do whatever you please, with no thought given to anyone else, or to confront every natural tendency, set aside personal preferences, and resist virtually every leaning of society by investing yourself in the strategies, values, and leadings of God? I argue (from personal experience and far too much failure) that compassion is more difficult to do than indifference; mercy is more challenging to practice than revenge; it takes more strength to be a person of peace than to be one of anger and violence; and that even though we might be most like God when we do it, one of the most wrenching decisions many people make is the decision to forgive a wound or offense.

Why is that kind of living so hard to do? Because it requires us to heed the warning Oswald Chambers offers in his December 9th contribution to *My Utmost for His Hightest:* "Beware of refusing to go to the funeral of your own independence." That's the funeral only the truly yielded person can attend, and the painful reality is, most of us just aren't that good at being yielded.

But it's not as though we don't have great examples. For instance:

Abraham Was Yielded

The biblical examples of people who lived by this spiritual value are many. Abraham certainly didn't grow up dreaming of leaving his home, extended family, and countrymen in order to go on a long, costly journey to a place the name of which he wasn't even told. But he did it, because he was yielded. Yes he was inspired by the promise and challenge of being a blessing to the entire world. But he was also yielded to the fact that he would have to leave many of those he loved most in order to see it happen. At about the age of seventy-five, with no address to punch into the Garmin and little idea what he would see whenever he and his troop finally got to where they were going, Abraham set off in yielded obedience "as the Lord had spoken to him." He, his wife, possessions, and people kept traveling until, as recorded in Genesis 11:7, God let him in on the fact that he had finally arrived at the territory that was to be his.

Abraham's tenure on Earth had its ups and downs. Like most of us, he had a messy life. His yieldedness was admirable, but it was also tainted by his humanity, chased by his fears, too often tilted by his insecurities, and sometimes interrupted during seasons of impatience. However, we must never forget that, at least in the Jewish, Muslim, and Christian traditions, Abraham is a person through whom we are all blessed. This is the man who, even when he didn't know exactly where he was being led, still went. It was Abraham who, after years of frustration while waiting for a son, dared to believe that even at their advanced ages, his wife Sarai could become pregnant and give him the child God had promised him.

How yielded was Abraham? Yielded enough to do the unthinkable—something not even the most spiritually mature people of faith I know would ever do. In response to his sense that God was testing him, Abraham set out to offer his son, Isaac, as a human sacrifice. While methodically sharpening his blade, Abraham commanded that long-awaited son to climb onto an altar, perhaps even assisting him by helping to adjust Isaac's weight as he wrapped him in the bindings that would hold him there.

"Is that too tight, my son?" Abraham might have asked while responding to yet another divine command about which he had not been given enough detail to feel comfortable. "I love you, son. I love you so very much" was certainly a sentiment deeply felt even if not verbalized as a reluctant but determined father looked to the near thicket in hopes that a substitute sacrifice would somehow appear.

"I see the altar, Father, but where's the ram for the offering?"

Abraham must have kept hearing that ringing question his trusting son asked him, almost gagging on the words as he responded, "God will provide the offering, Isaac. God will certainly provide it. Here now, step up here."

So confident and ready to follow was Abraham, scripture tells us, that he believed that even should no substitute sacrifice be provided and he be forced to drive that dreaded blade through the neck of his own child, God would immediately raise the young man back to life to stroll with his father back down the hill the same way they had ascended it, side by side, hand in quivering hand.

Abraham was yielded. He was willing to allow God to dictate his personal agenda. Sure, his yieldedness was intermittent. It wasn't perfectly executed—but nothing done on this journey toward healthy spirituality ever is, is it?

John the Baptizer Was Yielded

When John, the baptizer of Jesus, sat on his dad's knee and answered the question, "And what do you want to be when you grow up, John?" I doubt he looked into his father's eyes and, with a huge smile on his face, answered, "I want to do all sorts of great things for God and my people but never really get recognized for it, grow up living in the rugged and unforgiving wilderness, live on bugs and wear really uncomfortable, unfashionable clothes, then be imprisoned and eventually beheaded for something I didn't do." Yet, of course, that's exactly how things turned out for him. And they turned out that way simply because John was fully yielded.

Perhaps the climax of John's yieldedness can be seen through an indirect discussion he had with his cousin, Jesus. Christ and his apostles had been preaching and demonstrating the very things

John the baptizer spent his life preaching: that the Kingdom of God was at hand and here for the taking. People were experiencing healing in their bodies and the bodies of those close to them; the dead were being raised right out of their coffins while en route to the graveyard;[52] and the heat was being turned up with the message of Jesus and people's receptivity to it.

John, though, for no other reason than that he was the object of a powerful woman's incredible jealousy, was hearing about all of this from prison. Understandably, he began to entertain doubts. Things were not working out the way he had expected. The reign of God appeared to be slow in coming, at least in its fullness. King Herod was still on his throne, backed up by the power of the Roman governor Pontius Pilate and his imperial soldiers. John, instead of seeing God set the people of Israel free in triumph, was rotting in jail. He just *had* to ask the astounding question that had been worming its way into his mind and creeping up on his otherwise steady faith.

During a prison visit to bring food and catch him up on a number of things, John saw his chance to clear his haunted mind. Even though John had seen Jesus in action and heard from his own students that Jesus was still doing great things, he called two of them over and asked them to go and ask Jesus something. "Go and ask him this," John pleaded. "Ask, 'Are you the one who was to come, or should we expect someone else?'" So they went to Jesus and did exactly as John had instructed.[53]

It was a pretty straightforward question to a man incapable of telling anything but the truth. A simple yes or no was what John was looking for. That he would ask at all was a bit strange, though. Wasn't it John the baptizer who had dipped Jesus into the river when he was baptized? Hadn't John's entire life revolved around announcing the coming realization of God's dream for humanity (through Jesus) in the first place? And on that day when they did meet for Christ's baptism, didn't John make it very clear that he had actually been looking for Jesus to make himself known? At that time, John must have certainly recognized Jesus as the one sent by God, since he tried to talk Jesus out of being baptized by him, suggesting instead that it was he who should be the one submitting to baptism by *Jesus*. "I have need to be baptized by *YOU*, and do you come to me?" John had asked.[55]

But the strongest evidence of the fact that John should have already known who Jesus was might be in John 1:32-34. This text appears to remove all doubt about whether John had already been convinced that Jesus was Messiah. John had actually seen the Holy Spirit descend upon Jesus in the form of a dove and heard God verbally confirm the Messiahship of Jesus. He certainly had no questions about whether Jesus was the one he had been looking for *before* his unjust imprisonment. That much seems clear.

John invested his short but significant life announcing the pending arrival of Christ. And having recognized Jesus years earlier at the waters of baptism, then seeing the dove descending and hearing the heavenly voice of affirmation as that dove sat perched on the Lord's shoulder, how can there be any doubt in John's mind about whether or not Jesus was the one he had been looking for? How could he have asked such a shocking question . . . unless he was becoming worn and somehow discouraged by his captivity?

It seems reasonable to assume that John, like virtually everyone before him who had awaited the arrival of Israel's Messiah, was anticipating a more literal reign on the part of Jesus. And if the kingdom had actually come, John must have had the same question any of us would have asked had we found ourselves in prison knowing someone very close to us was now in power, with the authority and ability to release us. "If you're now the king, how much longer will it be before you take your throne and I'm freed so I can join you in the management of your people?" might have been the other question John was asking—the question within the question. And who could blame him?

Christ's unconventional response is strong evidence for his understanding of the level of John's yieldedness. After instructing John's messengers to simply report back to John what they had seen, Jesus adds a verbal message. "Blessed is anyone who does not stumble on account of me," he says. Did Jesus see in John's question a "stumbling" of sorts? If not, then why mention it at all? Could it have been that Jesus was preparing John for things that might lead to even further doubt? Was he really saying, "Hang in there, John. It's going to get a little darker before the light comes—both for you *and* for me"?

The effect of Christ's short response must have sounded like this in John's ears: "I'm not coming for you, dear cousin and faithful friend. However, there's no need for you to continue to look for someone else. Yes, I am he. What you saw and believed on the day you plunged me into the river is still true." So yielded was John that Jesus knew all he needed to hear was this: the blind were seeing, the lame were walking, and the good news was being received.

John was so submitted that this was the only answer he would require in order to reaffirm what he had believed and asserted on the day of that baptism. "Yes, I am indeed 'the one who was to come,'" John must have heard through Jesus's response, "and blessed are you if you are so surrendered that you can keep from stumbling over my decision to allow your suffering to continue and even accelerate in that terrible place."

Jesus spoke more highly about John than he did about any other human being. So impassioned was his affirmation of John that even today's reader can find it difficult not to blush while reading it.[56] But John never even heard what Jesus said. The text is clear about the fact that the disciples John sent to ask his question had already left by the time Jesus began that very encouraging discourse.

Sometime after that, the man Jesus referred to as being "as great as any person to have ever been born" was executed. As a direct result of his faithfulness and yieldedness to what was true, right, and just, the head of John the baptizer was brutally severed from his body and given as a party gift to a young girl who had danced particularly well and pleased her host.

Yieldedness is *THE WILLINGNESS TO ALLOW GOD TO DICTATE YOUR PERSONAL AGENDA.* And it takes an extraordinary person to practice it.

Interested in something more than a timid, safe spirituality? Then you'd better learn to yield.

Mary Was Yielded

When Beatle Paul McCartney wrote the words to the compelling ballad "Let It Be," he was, by his own report, thinking of his mom, Mary McCartney, who, sadly, died when he was just fourteen. But the refrain of that song echoes the sentiments of another famous "Mother Mary" as well. "Let it be" was also the response of Mary, the mother of Jesus, after the angel Gabriel visited her and told her that she was about to become pregnant with the savior of the world.

"Behold," she responded to her uninvited midnight guest, "I am the handmaid of the Lord; *LET IT BE* to me according to your word."[57]

Does anyone really believe it was easy for her to hear about what awaited her? Of course she was honored to have been chosen by God to carry and eventually give birth to the true king of Israel and the long-awaited rescuer of humankind. But that certainly wasn't a plot Mary had any hand in writing for herself. And it was most likely not one she would have chosen.

Put yourself in Mary's place. You're engaged to be married to Joseph and you know that you have kept yourself a virgin in anticipation of that day. Very soon you will be joined with him physically even as you already have been united officially and emotionally. Then, in the middle of the night, an angel—not just *any* angel, mind you, but the chief angel, Gabriel himself—appears to you as though standing right there next to your bed. You're convinced you must be dreaming. You shake your head, rub your eyes, slap your face, and look again. But he's still there, and now he's going to say something.

"Change of plans, blessed friend. You're soon going to realize that you are pregnant," he announces. Talk about ruining a good night's sleep!

"How can that be," you ask, "when, to the best of my knowledge, I've never had sex? Trust me, I'd remember something like that."

"So favored by God are you that, with all the young women in the world from which to choose, God has selected you to give birth to the person who will be the ultimate answer to every prayer that has ever been prayed."

You are shocked. How in the world can this be? And if it's true, how could it possibly be called a blessing—an expression of being "favored"? You're convinced Joseph won't believe you, your parents won't believe you, and the town elders won't believe you. Even your closest friends will never believe that the reason your belly is starting to swell is that God has planted in you the messianic zygote for which so many have been waiting. Now instead of looking forward to your wedding day and the celebration your family has been planning and saving for, all you can think of is certain discovery and possibly the public punishment reserved for fallen women.

No wonder the text describes Mary as having been "greatly troubled" and notes that she was "pondering what kind of salutation this might be."[58] All of us would be "pondering" that too!

Then, perhaps after trying several more times to wake yourself but failing each time, you, like Mary, decide to do what comes more and more naturally to those who are finding true and rich spirituality. You yield. "Behold, the bond slave of the Lord. Be it done to me according to your word."[59]

Unless God mercifully caused it, I doubt Mary found it easy to close her eyes that night. Rest didn't come any easier during the rest of Mary's life, either. She was forced to give birth while on the road, traveled long distances with her husband to hide from those who were trying to murder their son, probably spent at least part of Jesus's young years as a single parent, and finally, after a life of treasuring in her heart the promises and claims of the visiting angel on that sleepless night, watched as the son who had done nothing except love every person who crossed his path was arrested, mocked, tortured, crucified, and killed.

Mary has been appreciated, celebrated, consecrated, and even venerated because of the significance of her gift to the world. But as fantastic as her contribution was, it's important to remember that it was only possible because she was spiritually established enough to choose to allow herself to become a big part of that story. Mary knew the importance of being able to be led. She was spiritually great because she was yielded, willing to allow God to dictate her personal agenda.

Yieldedness, though, doesn't always play nice. It sometimes bites the hand that seeks it.

Danny Morris and Charles Olsen wrote a potentially disturbing paragraph while discussing the issue of allowing God to set the agenda and then responding to it. Noting how often they meet people who are actually afraid to be led by God, they say, "They fear that if God's will is done, it will result in hardship; that God's will has cutting edges and unhappy results. They fear that God's will may be the worst thing that could happen. Many people fear that God may require them to do almost impossible tasks. If a person asks God to reveal the divine will, he or she may have to quit his or her job, become a missionary, or sell that boat. An uneasy feeling lingers in the Church. Don't get too close to God. God will only make life difficult."[60]

It's not necessarily their point, but I'm still looking for the concerns mentioned in Morris and Olsen's statement that aren't at least potentially and/or occasionally true. Even that last line, "Don't get too close to God. God will only make life difficult," can at times *feel* true. It is a great and right thing to be yielded. But let's not be naïve. Like its cousin faith, yieldedness has a rent payment. In other words, it's a mistake to assume or expect that a person can practice yieldedness—allow God to dictate his or her personal agenda—and never face potentially challenging costs. The odds of diving into the surf and never getting wet might be substantially better.

It's a relatively light one when compared to some of the things faithful people around the world and throughout history have faced, but let me once again offer an example from our own family's life.

One June our family was grilling "Grecoburgers" (no, I can't give you the recipe, so please don't write and ask) in the backyard and celebrating our son Josh's birthday. Of course each of the kids had invited friends over for the feed. After we had eaten, our son came up to me and said that one of his guests hadn't had a shower in several days (I had already figured that out when his friend hugged me and thanked me for the meal) and asked if he might take one at our place before he left.

"Of course he can," I responded. "But are the showers broken at his house?"

"No, they're not broken at his house. He doesn't *have* a house. His parents kicked him out and he's been sleeping in the hedges at school, trying to finish so he can graduate with our class."

I couldn't believe what Josh was saying. We lived in the Denver suburbs, for crying out loud. Were there really homeless kids at Arvada West High School? A while later I asked my daughter if she knew anything about this scandal. Not only did she know, she added to the problem by pointing out one more of our dinner guests.

"He's also without a place to live," she whispered.

I just shook my head and did my best to close the ears of my heart. I knew enough about God to know that it was dangerous to make eye contact with him when there was human need nearby.

Two days later our number-two son and our daughter approached me and asked the question God had already floated in my mind. Could Rob move in with us just until the end of the term? That way, they explained, he might be able to graduate and get a scholarship to college. He could use David's room (our eldest was away at college). Besides, they went on, he was interested in being around a Christian family. He even said he wished he could investigate being a Christian.

They didn't have to wait long for my answer. My wife was in the middle of a very demanding degree program at the University of Colorado Medical Center and I was already giving my children far less of myself than I felt they needed or deserved. How could I add a troubled teen to our household, even though he was a pretty likable kid who was interested in God? I said no, reasoning that it was just not a well-thought-out request—one that was coming at a most inopportune time.

My "no," however, wasn't really very convincing. I kept tripping over the words of Jesus (mostly because the kids kept throwing them in front of me as I tried to walk). "I was homeless and you didn't house me. You closed up the empty spare bedroom I provided for you and let me sleep in the weeds only because logic (and the way you had things planned out) made no room for you to take the risk of inviting me in." The idea that it was so easy to claim friendship with Jesus but so difficult to treat a stray student the way Jesus would have treated him, or worse, would himself have wanted to have been treated, troubled me. As Archibald MacLeish put it in a piece entitled "JB," we had been:

> Chosen by the chance of seeing,
> By the accident of sight,
> By stumbling on the moment of it,
> Unprepared, unwarned, unready,
> Thinking of nothing, of his drink, of his bed,
> His belly, and it happens, and he sees it—
> Caught in that inextricable net,
> Of having witnessed, having seen—
> He alone.

I had seen. And through the chance act of having seen, I had been chosen for an "agenda adjustment." I was trapped by the invitation to yield and I knew it even before I had declined the offer. The observations of Ronald Rolheiser were haunting me even before I had read them. The practice of Christian spirituality (he uses the word Church but he seems to be saying the same thing) "puts a rope around us, takes away our freedom, and takes us where we would rather not, but should, go."[61]

Then there was the call from Canada, one I'm sure had been orchestrated by his mother and his siblings, where our eldest student/son "dared" me with the offer to give up his room so Rob could have a place to sleep. "Besides, Dad," he reminded, "it's a no-brainer. It's not what we planned, but it's what we need to do. He's sleeping in the bushes and we have an unused bed. You should let him move in. Even Mom agrees."

I knew the rest of the family was right. Rob moved in just before Christmas and nothing in our household was the same again.

Things with Rob are good now—*really* good—but some of the immediate outcomes of my yieldedness, reluctant and sour-hearted as it was, made life much more inconvenient. The house got messier, everything became more complicated, family conversations were more delicate, the "parental worry" level was elevated, and the food budget shot out of sight as an additional group of students began to drop by to see their friend's new place. The toughest thing, though, was that even though he had a place to sleep and shower, Rob, who to this day is a dear friend who is doing well with children of his own (one of whom is named after our Josh), didn't finish high school after all and struggled mightily before finally turning a more healthy corner in his life.[62]

The practice of yielding doesn't always escort the practitioner down the roughest road with the deepest ruts. It does, however, demand a willingness to navigate those kinds of roads—to endure real, even if only temporary, darkness. It's a darkness that leads to light, a darkness that is not wandered alone, a darkness sired by the dignity to which it will eventually yield, but it's darkness just the same.

Bernard of Clairvaux stings us with what he writes on this topic. "For that death, that opprobrium, that scorn, the beatings which Christ endured, what else were they but outstanding examples of obedience [*yieldedness*] for his body, that is, ourselves? . . . From what he suffered, then, we learn how it behooves us as just men to suffer deeply for the sake of obedience."[63]

There is a swarthy side of yieldedness, where at first glance the good rarely laugh and the children seldom dance. But it's in those gloomy back streets that genuine spirituality is both formed and found—when there exists acquiescence to the obligation to wander the tenebrous trails of honor in search of a divine silhouette.

Yieldedness has a dark side. But its dark never really stays dark. And a spiritual pilgrim who isn't willing to negotiate its murky trails can never be truly potent in the eyes of the God of light. That will only happen where there is an authentic willingness to endure the substantive, even if only temporary, sightlessness that sometimes attaches itself to the agenda of God.

The state of New Hampshire has a motto taken from a toast written by one of their most revered revolutionary war heroes, General John Stark: "Live free or die." Stark's point was a positive one, expressing his conviction that death was not necessarily the worst option a person could choose—especially when the alternative was to tolerate tyranny and evil. In fact, a more complete version of Stark's quote is, "Live free or die. Death is not the worst of evils."

Unlike General Stark, I've never had to test the true level of my convictions by being willing to place my life on the line for them. So far all I've been called to do is to remain grateful that he, and those who stood next to him in battle, were willing. I fear, however, that were Stark to see how those words, penned in the early nineteenth century as part of a celebration of his greatest victory, were sometimes used today, he might be as sad now as he was happy on the day he offered them. For the phrase "live free or die" has, by some, been removed from its original context of mutual dependence, contribution, and sacrifice for the sake of a worthy cause, and implanted instead as justification for the right to live a life that depends upon no one and offers nothing to others.

The phrase "live free or die" could never have been meant by its author to mean that a person had no authority greater than him or herself. Were that his point, Stark could never have dared to order his troops or command his subordinates with any expectation that they should listen to him. If "live free or die" was meant to endorse the notion that every and any individual could do whatever he or she wanted with no concern for the effects their decisions might have on others, then one of America's great commanders was implying that he won one of the most strategic military battles of the American Revolution by means of some sort of ingenious military chaos, where "each man did that which was right in his own eyes" and things just sort of worked out for the best. Even when your troops outnumber those of your enemy two to one, as was the case with Stark, the unwillingness to be led will always result in a resounding defeat.

"Live free or die" is a truly great phrase and an even greater concept. But when by the word "free" we actually mean "never give way," "never submit," "never be led," "never yield," "live life 'my way,'" then in order to be fair to the inevitable results of such a life, one of the words must be changed. For when that happens, "live free or die" is guaranteed to become "live free *and* die."

Thomas A. Kempis wrote, "And he is truly learned, who renounces his own will for the will of God."[64] In other words, contrary to what so many believe, though "My Way" is the easier way, it's not the most dynamic way. "*Thy* will be done" is a much more dangerous, demanding prayer than "*My* will be done." It takes a far more substantial, confident, adventurous, and spiritually deep person to yield—to allow God to call the shots.

That, at least, is the way I see it. And I remain convinced that most of those reading this either already are or will soon become likewise convinced, coming to the same conclusion as one of the greatest and most well-known leaders of the modern Christian world when he said, "I resolved to dedicate all my life to God; all my thoughts, and words, and actions; being thoroughly convinced there was no medium, but that every part of my life (not some only) must either be a sacrifice to God, or myself."[65]

That's yieldedness—*THE WILLINGNESS TO ALLOW GOD TO DICTATE YOUR PERSONAL AGENDA.*

A prayer for the well planned:

"You know what I'm good at, Lord? I'm good at making a plan and then asking You to bless it. And I'm frighteningly good at calling that 'yieldedness' too. I'm not asking You to completely erase my ability to strategize. In fact, I'd love it if You would strengthen it. What I am asking for is that You would show me the kindness of always jumping line when my plans look a lot more holy than they actually are. Your plans must not merely cooperate with mine, they must trump them. So kill yet again, God. Kill the notion in me that just because I prayed before I planned, the plan I came up with was first born in Heaven; kill any unhealthy dependence upon my own logic and understanding; kill everything that competes with Your anything. Tug on my leash and holler 'Heel' when I step out ahead of You. For otherwise, I fear I always will step out. Amen."

NOTES

CHAPTER EIGHT
LOYALTY

There must be a spiritual attachment in loyalty in order for it to truly represent its intended enduring value.

LOYALTY:

The Williness to Live As Though Yesterday Was Watching,
And Tomorrow Had a Vote

All over London there are signs that remind you just how dangerous it can be to cross a street. In London's case, of course, it has to do with the fact that so many of the tourists who visit that grand city come from places where people drive on the right side of the road and, therefore, have learned over a lifetime of stepping into crosswalks to look first to the left (for oncoming traffic) before stepping off the sidewalk. It's surprising how difficult it is to break that habit, especially if it's just for a one or two-week vacation. That's where those reminders come in—for painted on the curb of just about every major street in London are the words, "Look Right ----->." In London, of course, people drive in the left lane.

Still, every time I visit London I come home surprised that I didn't get run over by a double-decker bus. Even with all those painted reminders, I revert. With each close call I remember one of the childhood lessons my mom taught me about streets. The earliest of all, of course, was that we shouldn't even go NEAR a street. "There are magic, invisible snakes in the street," I was told, "and the minute you step off the curb without an adult holding your hand, they will appear from nowhere and bite you on the foot." Worked for me. But as I got older and began to walk to school, a more verifiable version of that same law was drilled into me. It was the same rule that was drilled into the rest of the kids of the developed world: "Always look both ways before crossing the street."

Who knows how many lives that one simple rule has saved or how much "guardian angel overtime" it has made unnecessary? It's a good lesson, a good rule, and a good practice to continue throughout life. But it's also a good illustration for this chapter on loyalty. For in a sense, the loyalty we'll discuss here as a characteristic of true and compelling spirituality is a bit like walking across a busy street.

Albert Einstein seemed to have been captured by an appreciation of a debt he owed and his responsibility to look both ways to repay it when he said, "Many times a day, I realize how much my outer and inner life is built upon the labors of people, both living and dead, and how earnestly I must exert myself in order to give in return as much as I have received." In other words, our expressions of loyalty are connected to decisions we make in the present, but in all the choices of life there is traffic coming from at least two directions: the past (which is what most of us think of when we consider the challenge to remain loyal—honoring our past) and the future (which, though as important as the past, often gets much less consideration). The tension seems to grow even more, Einstein implies, as we involve names and faces.

Though my experience of it is far less dramatic and far-reaching, I feel Einstein's word very deeply. For instance, how can I make a leadership decision in my church without remembering my Aunt Peachie and Uncle Lenny, who were instrumental in me finding faith; Pastor Wayne Adams, who was the first preacher who ever caused me to consider the crazy possibility that a sermon could actually be interesting; or my homiletics professor,

Jim Andrews, who so deeply stamped the need for pastoral relevance and passion into me that I still hear his challenges in my sleep?

On the other hand, those who have gone before me are only half of the story. The trusting eyes of the children I see daily remind me that there are powerless, dependent innocents who unknowingly depend upon me to make choices that serve them too. Grandchildren, nieces, nephews, and even the yet-to-be-conceived kings and queens of tomorow "call" for their rightful place of influence on the resolutions we make today.

In short, loyalty demands that we consider both the past *and* the future before stepping into the traffic of current decisions. Loyalty ALWAYS looks both ways.

Let's look at an excellent example of someone who not only understands this very clearly, but has come to that understanding at substantial personal cost.

A film that was originally scheduled to be released in 2012 tells the story of a Burmese democracy advocate and leader. It's the account of an amazing woman, a modern-day, Burmese combination of Joan of Arc, Mahatma Gandhi, and Nelson Mandela. Her name is San Suu Kyi. And the experiences attached to that name are astounding, to say the least.

San Suu Kyi was Oxford educated, receiving a B.A. after studies in philosophy, politics, and economics. In 1972 she was married to Tibetan expert Michael Aris. In 1988, while her husband stayed behind to care for their two sons, San Suu Kyi returned to Burma to care for her ailing mother. While there, she became smitten with the people of her homeland as they openly protested the oppression that had become a regular part of Burmese life and publically expressed their yearning for freedom.

That San Suu Kyi would be drawn into her people's movement seems to have been inevitable. At the age of two, her father, a general who was a leading advocate for democracy (referred to as "Burma's independence hero") was assassinated because of his political views and the independence movement he led. For San Suu Kyi to see that even though her father had died, the principles and dreams for which he lived had not, stirred her heart mightily. It wasn't long before she was speaking at large rallies and picking up where her dad had left off. As a direct result of this decision to openly involve herself in the cause that had cost her parents so dearly, San Suu Kyi's life, though full of purpose, became quite difficult. Consider the following:

- She spent fifteen of her first twenty-two years back in Burma under strict house arrest. Of course, she always happened to be confined at key times during election years.
- She had to endure the pain of knowing her leadership contributed to the military's decision to try to silence the movement by killing thousands of protestors.
- At an incident during her campaign for democracy she is reported to have courageously walked toward soldiers aiming rifles directly at her.
- San Suu Kyi was mercilessly misrepresented and discredited in the government-controlled press and, though she was general secretary of her organization, the National League

for Democracy, she was illegally banned from running for office when elections were finally held.

- She watched as her National League for Democracy won more than 80% of the popular vote, then endured the anguish that resulted when the results of the election were never recognized by the military regime that held power, and the disappointment when the reins of leadership were never relinquished.
- She was illegally held under house arrest by the Burmese government for five years after the election won by her party. And even when she was finally released in 1995, her rights to travel were severely and forcefully restricted.
- During a subsequent detainment, cancer took her husband's life. At the time of his death it had been almost five years since they had seen each other. When he petitioned the Burmese government to visit his wife one last time before he died, he was turned down. Instead San Suu Kyi was encouraged by the government to leave Burma and travel to England if she wanted to see her husband. However, she knew that if she left, she would never be allowed to return. So San Suu Kyi made the tortured decision to remain in custody.
- After husband Michael's death, San Suu Kyi was briefly released. However, her "freedom" was short-lived. She was soon placed under house arrest again for trying to leave the capital city of Rangoon to participate in political meetings in other regions of the country.
- Though eventually released again, this time with permission to travel and speak as a result of an agreement negotiated by the United Nations, the meetings she held were disrupted by government forces.
- In 2003 there was an assassination attempt on her life. Though she survived, more than seventy of her supporters didn't. The attack (where many of those seventy-plus lovers

of freedom were beaten to death) was eventually referred to as "The Depayin Massacre." The United Nations called for an investigation, but one was never done.

- After that failed attempt on her life, San Suu Kyi was once again placed under house arrest. This time, though, her phone lines were cut, her mail was stopped, and protective security at her compound was removed. So strict were prohibitions on visitors during that incarceration that at one point even the U.N. Secretary General was denied an audience.
- Then, in 2009, just days before house arrest was due to expire, San Suu Kyi was officially arrested and charged with breaking the conditions of her detainment after an American citizen entered her home and refused to leave. Because of this she was convicted and sentenced to three years in prison. Under pressure, this was reduced to eighteen more months of house arrest, ensuring that, yet again, San Suu Kyi would be detained until after public elections had taken place.
- In 2010 the National League for Democracy, the party she helped to form, was officially banned by the regime. And at the end of that year she was finally given the freedom to leave her home.

All of this leads to an obvious question: What in the world would drive a person to make such severe sacrifices?

It wasn't a need for public recognition, or celebrity, or some of the financial gains that often come with it. San Suu Kyi already had plenty of that. She won the Sakharov Prize, the European parliament's award for human rights, and was presented the Presidential Medal of Freedom by President Clinton. But she wasn't able to be there to receive either one, leaving that up to her husband and sons. And when she won the 1991 Nobel Peace Prize, she chose to use the $1.3 million that came with the award to establish a health and education trust for the people of Burma rather than to make life easier for herself or to better her political career. No, recognition was and still is not her motivator.

What would compel a person to have feelings so strong that she would plead with people around the world to "please use your liberty to promote ours"? Why would someone who didn't really have to be so willing to live apart from the spouse she loved, the sons she bore, and the grandchildren she unquestionably longed to hold? How is it possible that as many as seventeen years before she returned to Burma, and the year before she was married to him, San Suu Kyi could feel inclined to write to her fiancé, Michael Aris, "I only ask one thing, that should my people need me, you would help me to do my duty by them"— especially when, in that same post she said, "Sometimes I am beset by fears that circumstances and national considerations might tear us apart just when we are so happy in each other that separation would be a torment."[66] Political convictions? Obviously. Love for the people of Burma? Of course. Religious values attached to her Buddhist beliefs? Without question. But other things San Suu Kyi said and wrote imply that a far deeper root, a much more binding and severe form of loyalty also drove her.

Apparently, San Suu Kyi felt she owed something to the parents who had gone before her—specifically her father, Burmese independence hero General Aung San, who helped achieve independence for Burma in the early twentieth century and, as previously noted, was ultimately assassinated in 1947. She seemed to have inherited from her hero father not only his sense of loyalty to Burma's people and their quest for freedom, but also his profound willingness to suffer with them during that quest. San Suu Kyi described her father as "a man who put the interests of the country before his own needs, who remained poor and unassuming at the height of his power, who accepted the responsibilities of leadership without hankering after the privileges."[67] She obviously admired those traits and adopted them for herself.

In her first and best-known speech at the famous Shwedagon Pagoda in central Yangon on August 26, 1988, San Suu Kyi revealed that loyalty when she said, "The present crisis is the concern of the entire nation. *I could not, as my father's daughter, remain indifferent to all that was going on. This national crisis could, in fact, be called the second struggle for independence.*"[68]

This wasn't a loyalty that came upon her late in life, either. Even before she was particularly "political," a longtime friend from India said that during her Oxford years in the eighties, San Suu Kyi always used to say, "I can never forget whose daughter I am." And in the foreword to her book, *Freedom from Fear,* San Suu Kui cautions that when the time came that her country and her people needed her, she would have to return.[69] In fact, she went so far as to vow that she would *"serve Burma unto death like her parents did."*[70]

San Suu Kyi made decisions with which I'm sure not everyone would agree. The stuff that boiled in her and her determination to be led by it meant she and her husband lived on opposite sides of the globe and her sons grew up without the presence and direct influence of their mother. Her outspoken quest for the freedom of Burma's people resulted in her being sequestered from the very ones she sought to help. As a Christian, I obviously have significant differences of conviction and major disagreement with her Buddhist faith around many theological matters. No question. All of that notwithstanding, her life is a wonderful illustration of the focus of this chapter. And I respect her for it.

San Suu Kyi possesses what some classify as a virtue. She's acutely aware of a sense of debt—the notion that she owes something to those who have gone before her. She lives with loyalty: *THE WILLINGNESS TO LIVE AS THOUGH YESTERDAY WAS WATCHING.*

But San Suu Kyi's loyalty doesn't just look to the past for its sustenance. She also lives with an understanding that those who come after her deserve a say in their future. Her decisions reflect a conviction that when it comes to today's decisions, *TOMORROW HAS A VOTE.*

"We are against violence because we think violence begets violence. And we look at it with a long-term point of view. We are not looking at it just in terms of the next month or the next year. We are looking at it in terms of the future of our country, and we think that for the future of our country it is not a good idea to encourage violence."[71] So not only does San Suu Kyi's sense of loyalty look back through lenses of debt owed to her parents, but also forward through a sense of obligation today's decision-makers have to an otherwise voiceless tomorrow.

Loyalty always does that—it does its best to listen to what tomorrow might have to say about the decisions today makes. A good practice, when you stop and think about it—especially since it's often those who follow us who are stuck with the results (both good and bad) of the things we choose to do or not do. San Suu Kyi understands this, and she has suffered for that understanding.

Her tenacity has begun to pay off, though. According to a recent *Wall Street Journal* article,[72] the ice in Burma is melting. In April of 2012 open elections were held to fill vacant seats in parliament. In the months leading up to those elections, hundreds of political prisoners, including some of the most outspoken and popular, were released. And because of what they saw, though cautious at first, many countries (including the United States) relaxed the restrictions they had placed on trade and relations with Burma. In fact, following the 2012 elections, the U.S. restored diplomatic relations with the formerly isolated nation and lifted sanctions that had banned trade with Myanmar.

Oh, and among the newly elected officials sworn into parliament in the once rogue nation was one San Suu Kyi, finally allowed to take office.

Without resorting to the violence that always seems to stain generations who never chose to live by it, San Suu Kyi and other reformers who also made decisions with the future in mind seem to have made great gains toward the changes for which they sacrificed so much. Like the wise pedestrian who knows one must look both ways before moving forward to cross a busy street, democracy advocates in one of the most resistant and oppressive countries of our time have remained loyal. But theirs hasn't been a one-dimensional "loyalty." They have understood that *LOYALTY IS THE WILLINGNESS TO LIVE AS THOUGH YESTERDAY WAS WATCHING, AND TOMORROW HAD A VOTE.*

As wonderful and inspiring as it is to have such a compelling example of this definition of loyalty in an historical contemporary like San Suu Kyi, the question of loyalty being a spiritual virtue still lingers. After all, though most would agree loyalty is generally a good quality in a person, we can also agree that it can and often is misapplied. For instance, loyalty to the cause of justice that is expressed through advocacy for oppressed people is an honorable thing. But loyalty to fellow gang members—especially when expressed through crime and violence—certainly is not. There must be a spiritual attachment in loyalty (and not necessarily a conscious one, I suspect) in order for it to truly represent its intended enduring value, an employment of it that parallels or contributes to the values of God and, in some way, His agenda for all of creation.

Biblical examples of that spiritual attachment are embedded in the lives of just about every major hero in the Bible. Here are just a few examples of the kind of loyalty that "looks both ways" before stepping into the streets of decision:

Like San Suu Kyi, the biblical heroes listed in Hebrews 11 suffered for their loyalty. Already noted as an example of yieldedness, in Hebrews 11:8-10 Abraham is also a pretty strong spokesman for loyalty. There he looks back to the promise of God and clings to it while also looking forward to what the Bible calls "a different city," with foundations whose architect and builder is God Himself. Abraham looked both ways; throughout his life he looked back at the guarantees and instructions of God while also looking forward to the future his obedience would build for his descendants. His spiritual development was approaching the point where he had begun to make decisions as though yesterday was watching and tomorrow had a vote.

Hebrews 11:39 can initially be something of a discouragement. After reading a list of famous names (some attached to people who, precisely because of the same faith that brought them God's royal affirmation, endured some of the most gruesome examples of cruelty ever recorded), we are reminded that none of these great ones received what had been promised them. But then the text almost seems to amend itself by noting that there is some connection between them (the faithful ones) and us, as though their promises were fulfilled or made complete in *our* experiences. Astonishing!

Is the Bible implying here that an ancient saint looks back at the promises of God and, in the face of terrible suffering and torture, refuses to give up on them, all the while believing those promises will be fulfilled through his or her descendants? Is the Bible's sense of loyalty being something that looks both ways that severe? If so, that's a type of loyalty I've yet to offer anyone or experience myself. Imagine being chained to a wall while a saw is laid across your abdomen and the first slices of your torn flesh become lodged in its dull, rusty blades. Who but the most splendid among us would still be able to say to God in that moment, "I consider a promise kept through my great-great-great-grandchildren to be a promise kept to me"? If that isn't proof that the grand ones of scripture were loyal both to their past *and* their extended future, then I don't know what is.

Hebrews 12:1-2 ties this all together. There the Bible as much as says, "Look back to those who have gone before you and handed you the faith you now hold in your hearts. In fact, look around you, for they are still with you, still encouraging you." Then, just after the presentation of a stirring and dramatic invitation to that retrospective, the writer of Hebrews calls us to look both ways. "Run the race that is marked out for you with both an awareness of those who have gone before you (since they're watching over their investment in you) and the one who waits for you to cross your given finish line." In other words, "When you run, be loyal both to those who have handed you the baton of faith and the God to whom you will return it in the future, when your race concludes."

The study of loyalty in the life of Moses is certainly an interesting one. His mother sure seems to have understood it, risking her infant child's life by placing him in a small, waterproof basket, then floating him past the daughter of the Pharaoh in hopes that she would rescue him from the death order that had been directed toward all male Hebrew children. In doing that, Moses's mother (known only as "a Levite woman") showed an advanced level of loyalty, acting both in response to the values of the faith into which she had been born and the future of her people.

Hers was a faithful loyalty that paid off, too. Pharaoh's daughter did, indeed, take Moses and raise him as her own son.

As a favored member of the royal family, Moses was afforded many opportunities to confront the issue of loyalty as well. His most infamous moment came when, while enjoying the benefits of royal Egyptian privilege, he came upon a Hebrew slave being beaten by his Egyptian handler. Then, in an episode of confused loyalties that expressed itself through a fit of rage, Moses made a decision that changed his life dramatically. Not only did he stop the beating and rescue the slave, but killed the bully, then buried him in a shallow grave.

While in exile (because of that murder), Moses took for himself a wife and, through her, a new family with, of course, a new patriarch. Moses was committed to his father-in-law and served him for decades before a reluctant return to Egypt. And how could Moses be mentioned without a reference to one of the most well-known stories of all time: the story of the burning bush? There God, during Moses's career as a shepherd, asked Moses to be loyal to *Him* by returning to Egypt and delivering the Jewish people from centuries of slavery.

Moses as a man who practiced loyalty by our definition, though, is perhaps best seen near the end of his life. By the time we read his words as recorded in Deuteronomy 33, Moses has successfully led the Hebrew nation out of slavery, outmaneuvered the world's leading military, managed those millions of former slaves as they wandered as a sort of "nomad nation" through the wilderness, and guided them to the historical crescendo commonly known as "the entrance to the Promised Land."

Everything Moses worked and suffered for his entire adult life was finally there to be experienced; then word came that he would not be entering that land with his people. The honor of leading them in, he was told, would be handed off to two of his young apprentices. His response revealed his good and loyal heart.

Shortly after hearing that he wouldn't be allowed to walk in the land toward which he had been leading his people for decades, Moses did not protest. Nor did he complain. Instead, he remembered his past and blessed those who would enjoy the fruits of his years of faithful toil. Deuteronomy 33:29 records that blessing.

"May the Lord bless His land with the precious dew from Heaven above and with the deep waters that lie below," he said, "with the best the sun brings forth and the finest the moon can yield; with the choicest gifts of the ancient mountains and the fruitfulness of the everlasting hills; with the best gifts of the earth and its fullness and the favor of Him who dwelt in the burning bush."

That's right: Moses looked both ways. He prayed for tomorrow based on his remembrance of an event he had experienced yesterday. Then, after seeing the Promised Land and blessing those who would carry Israel into a future for which he paved the way with his own tears, Moses received God's assurance that his task had been successfully completed, sat down, and died.

In the Bible, Moses is known for his extraordinary humility. He was "the most humble man on the face of the earth," in fact, according to Numbers 12:3. In his life, he had been allowed to see God (well, everything but God's face), and unlike any other prophet in history, Moses spoke to God, as God Himself phrased it, "mouth to mouth." But even though all that was true of this great man, at the end of his life the most astounding quality he displayed might just be his incredible loyalty—his ability to live as though yesterday was watching and tomorrow had a vote. Obviously Moses knew he was part of a plan that went well beyond himself. Maybe that's why he refused to do anything that might hinder that plan's progress into the future—even a future that didn't include him.

It stands to reason that if the idea of looking both ways before crossing into a decision were a common biblical theme and practice, we would see it in the life and career of Jesus. In fact, if we didn't see it in him, the entire argument for it would fail, or at least lose considerable steam. Fortunately, that's not the case. Christ was loyal in every good sense of the word. Here are just a few examples, not necessarily the strongest ones, of how he showed loyalty's connection to the past and future of human history.

In Luke 4, Jesus's visit to the synagogue in Nazareth is recorded. There he reads from the book of Isaiah, initially astounding the hearers with his eloquent and articulate presentation. What happens next, though, is the focus here. After reading a text that's firmly planted in the historical past and the ministry of Isaiah, Jesus identifies himself with it. "Today this scripture has been fulfilled in your hearing." Immediately after looking back to Isaiah, Jesus spoils the moment, not to mention the mood, by implying that there's more to Isaiah's prophecy than just remembering the past and feeling good about being Jewish. In reminding his hearers that Isaiah's actual work was not limited to the blessing of Israel, Jesus in effect says that *his* won't be, either. Jesus not only remembers, but he also anticipates. He clarifies that God desires to bless the entire earth and every ethnicity on the face of it. He's not only looking back to Isaiah, but forward to what God ultimately has in mind for everything and everyone He created.

John 8 also displays a bit of this "looking both ways" idea. It begins with the story of the woman caught in adultery and the famous account of Jesus writing in the sand. It ends with Jesus offering some fairly challenging words to a group of people who had actually believed much of what he had been teaching. What is of greatest interest for purposes of the topic of "looking both ways," though, is the undercurrent of all that happens. Throughout the chapter Jesus refers back to his father and the instructions he receives from him. But whenever he does that it's with a link to the future as well. For instance, in verse 8:14 Jesus (in defense of a statement he made about himself) says, "I know where I've come from and where I am going." Of course he did, because Jesus always thought in terms of the past *and* the future.

A more extreme example of "looking both ways" comes just before the crowd again decides that Jesus must be permanently silenced. It shows up through a statement that seems to almost trump the very concept of time itself. "Before Abraham was born, I am," says Jesus. Talk about "looking both ways." Jesus looks both ways *at the same time.* He was, is, and always will be. Getting a headache yet?

One last compelling example of Jesus being loyal to both past and future comes in that final exhortation of the opening section of Hebrews 12. The first half of verse 2 reminds us that he, as both pioneer, author, and the one sent by God the Father to perfect or finish personal faith, made decisions during his earthly tenure with the past in mind. However, in the second half of that same verse, we're asked to recall that during those times when Jesus was suffering most, one of the things that gave him strength to move forward was a sense of duty to what was yet to come.

Jesus was loyal. He made choices based on what he had been called to do before he entered earth's history as a human practitioner AND what he knew to be in the best interest of those who would enter it after him. That, by the way, must be a big part of why the Bible links his suffering with the idea of "the joy set before him"—that joy being the redemption of those who, because of his life, death, and resurrection, would realize their need for the gift he was, and still *is*.

I pause even during the writing of this paragraph to consider how that must have worked in his "fully but not exclusively" human mind: when his heart suffered the deep pain of rejection—even betrayal by those he loved and came to help; when religious leaders who had been given the blessing of preparing the hearts of people to recognize and receive him were sometimes among those who rallied confused crowds to call for his rejection and eventual crucifixion; after his arrest, each time layers of skin were ripped open by a whip specially designed to maim but not kill, every strike leaving his torso looking more like it had just emerged from a burlap sack full of bobcats; when from the cross he heard, not for the first time, challenges tempting him to misuse his power for his own, temporary gain. In those moments, what was it that gave Jesus the strength to stick with the original plan instead of taking an early, much easier exit? What was it that so strengthened his resolve?

According to Hebrews 12, it was that "joy that was set before him"—the awareness that only if he remained willing to choose death over life would every single human being on earth eventually have the option to choose life over death. Apparently, our making that choice is what brings God his greatest pleasure. No wonder the love God has for all of humankind is so often referred to in the Bible as "loyal love." How could it be known as anything else when it was (and still is) practiced with such a perfect understanding of both past and future history?

Jesus was the epitome of "loyal." He lived *AS THOUGH YESTERDAY—THE PAST—WAS WATCHING AND TOMORROW—THE FUTURE—HAD A VOTE.*

My siblings and I buried our mom in October of 2011, just a little more than ten years after our dad was laid to rest. Dad's death was a shock, like a sucker-punch none of us was prepared to receive. Mom's was one we sadly and reluctantly welcomed after years of watching her decline at the hands of a debilitating, degenerative disease. Since both of their lives were so marked by this idea of loyalty, it's only fitting that my memories of them be bound to it too.

I preached my dad's funeral message. The text was taken from Ephesians 4:1, the sermonic theme being, "Live a life worthy of the lives lived for you." The idea was one that crept up on me through my grief. I began to think things like, *My life is an extension of my dad's life—of the life of every person who has ever invested in me, really. I owe something to my heritage, and to the heritage of those who will follow me.*

As expressed by Dan Folgelberg in his tribute to his own dad, I had become "a living legacy to the leader of the band." I owed it to him to live a life that was: 1) worthy of all that had been entrusted to me, and 2) would inspire in my own children that same healthy sense of debt.

As I prepared Dad's funeral message, I recalled one day with him in particular. It was summer in Sacramento, sometime in the early nineties during a family vacation trip from the church I was planting in Portland, Oregon. Dad and I were a twosome on the golf course, and he was teeing off first. As I stood behind him leaning on my driver, I noticed a few things: his grip was too strong; his pants didn't really match his shirt; his old British racing style, "snap down in the front" cap was "classic white with grease marks on the bill;" and his golf shoes were circa 1965 black (with white socks, of course). Yet, in spite of all that, I was sure I had never seen a finer-looking man in my life.

Suddenly my cheeks went fuzzy, my nose began to run, and I gave way to one of those gentle, quiet weepings that follow an experience of seeing true beauty. Then, just as he was getting ready to take his backswing, I stopped him.

"Hold up, Dad. Wait."

"Why? Was I doing something wrong?"

"No." I said as I walked up to him, just the two of us on the tee.

"Hey, kid . . . what's going on? You crying? You okay?"

"Nothing's wrong," I said. "It's just that while you were in that terrible stance, with that awful grip of yours, I was reminded of what a great father you've been to me. How in the world will I ever be able to say thank you? How could I ever pay you back for that?"

His response sort of shocked me. It was a "look both ways" response.

"Be an even better father to my grandchildren than I was to you," he said. Then for good measure he threw in a rider: "And be good to Brenda. Keep your vows."

Loyalty was a huge theme in my dad's life, so we made it *the* theme at his memorial too. But his wasn't a one-dimensional kind of loyalty. For him, loyalty not only looked back, but forward as well. It looked both ways.

When our mom died a decade later, the same could have easily been said of her passion for loyalty. We tried to capture that in the tribute to her that we posted in the *Oregonian* newspaper after her death.

"No matter how badly you had soiled your life, you knew that Aunt Carol still loved you; even when you fully deserved all you were getting, Mom could be counted on to knock on the door halfway through a whipping you had certainly earned, resulting in Dad cutting it shorter than it should have been; when you didn't have enough money to pay for your cut and perm, she suddenly remembered that she was running a special that day on cuts and perms; if she suspected you wanted a second steak, she was coincidentally 'not hungry' that evening; and when your boyfriend had broken up with you or your parents were driving you crazy, Grandma Greco (whether she was your biological grandmother or not) somehow knew just what you needed to hear in order to feel whole again."

Most would say of our mom what is said of many great moms: that she was, to use an old but effective cliché, "loyal to a fault." But though dependable and tenacious, it wasn't our *mom's* loyalty that stood out to me in her decline and ultimate death; it was that of my siblings—my sister Susan and brother

Lenny. For as our mom, once strong, decisive, and somewhat independent, began to succumb to the scarring demands of multiple sclerosis, it was my siblings who rose to the levels of loyalty we had all been raised to practice.

As her illness progressed, our mom expressed a desire to remain in her own home for as long as possible. When her health continued to decline and it became clear that she would have to be moved to a full-time care facility, it was my brother and sister who, in order to honor her wish, decided to take turns staying overnight at Mom's place instead. Daily and even through the night, they administered her meds and made sure she had all she needed, including good company. Though both of them had families and careers of their own, this became their chosen routine: alternating twenty-four-hour shifts, day after day, for the last several months of our mother's life.

My siblings and I talked about this, of course, me expressing my concern for them and my own sense of guilt for living six hundred miles away and not being able to do my share. But every time I suggested we find another way to care for our mom, my brother and sister responded with a "looking both ways" sense of loyalty.

"This is what she did for us all her life," they would argue. "Plus, this is what Dad would want us to do. It honors him too. Besides," and I think this was rich, "our kids all need to see what a real family looks like in order to have a chance at one for themselves someday."

Those weren't the exact words used, but they were pretty close, and the values expressed in them are dead on. To Susan and Lenny, every day (and night) spent caring for our mom was a day spent being loyal, with a clear sense that both those who had gone before and those who would next carry the torch of our family's faith were all looking on and would someday need to draw upon what they had seen.

LOYALTY IS THE WILLINGNESS TO LIVE AS THOUGH YESTERDAY WAS WATCHING, AND TOMORROW HAD A VOTE. And there is very little that's worth having in a spirituality that neglects the practice of it.

A prayer for those who are too focused on today:

"Lord, this is difficult for me. Yesterday is responsible for much of the trouble I experience today and tomorrow will offer little support for me the next time I'm challenged during a performance evaluation. I'm loyal to today, God . . . because today is where I have to live and survive. Today is what pays the bills and feeds the ego. Please heal the brokenness and frustration I sometimes feel when I encounter 'yesterday.' And give me a fresh vision for the importance of legacy— the power of a healthy handoff when I dream of how I might invest in 'tomorrow.' I want to be your servant, God, but I fear that I'm a bit too unwilling to serve unless that service results in something that directly benefits me. It's a painful admission, but that selfishness needs to go. Please inject it with a fatal dose of irrelevance and me with a life-giving shot of heavenly perspective. Recreate in me true loyalty. Amen."

SOME FINAL THOUGHTS

*Hold out for a sturdy, compelling spirituality
and reject all invitations to anything less.*

SOME FINAL THOUGHTS

I n life, I've noticed that sometimes the most internally
powerful people can appear to be among the weakest.
Spiritual depth is strange that way—like a finely tuned,
overbuilt NASCAR engine hidden under the hood of a
frumpy-looking, oxidized minivan. And like that minivan,
the well-developed spiritual heart is content to be faithful
in unremarkable daily service. Yet it remains fully capable
of blowing the doors off of much newer and shinier models
whenever the flag drops or the green light flashes.

My friend Nola was like that: an unimpressive exterior that
housed more spiritual horsepower than most drivers could
ever handle. She was only twelve or thirteen when she died.
But while she lived she was a master at cutting through gruff,
seemingly unapproachable exteriors with strong, soft, powerful,
tender love. It was as though she had been soaking in God's
brine all of her short life—permeated by divine seasonings, then
dressed with some sort of sanctified "special sauce" for the
enjoyment of anyone who had the good fortune to be around her.

I won't even try to remember the number of times she rolled
up alongside some stoic stranger in a park or forlorn-looking
person in a worship service and, in her well-worn, gravely voice,
asked what was wrong, then if they might like her to pray for
them or give them what she playfully referred to as one of her
"power hugs."

Friendship with Nola was like squaring up a fastball on the
first at-bat of a new season; it was like finally being asked to

the prom by that one particular love interest, or the feeling you get when you wake up in the morning and realize that the absolutely tragic thing that happened to you really was just a dream after all.

I was Nola's theologically trained pastor and almost four times her age when we worshipped together. She, on the other hand, had barely stepped through the front door of her life and certainly hadn't yet compiled a very impressive professional résumé. But weak as she appeared to be, I was sometimes intimidated by the depth and force of her faith.

Nola was frail, but she was strong; was tethered to a wheelchair, but nimble; had only ever experienced God through the lenses of a crippling disease, but manifested Him in ways I can only hope to realize someday. There was nothing that appeared to be particularly fancy, flashy, or contemporary about Nola. But, to put it in the street vernacular with which I began this book, Nola was a young lady with the kick-ass spirituality to which so many of us aspire. She was humble, yielded, teachable, celibate, loyal, faithful, and certainly courageous. Those ancient qualities so many of her contemporaries had foolishly traded for shinier but lesser traits had found a home in Nola. And through her unassuming example, I'm blessed to have been captured by a hunger for them too.

John was like that as well. I had served his wife, Anna, communion on one of her last clear-minded days. It was powerful, but in a tender, quiet way: her daughter there to hold her up in bed, with me offering sour juice and stale bread as poor substitutes for what they actually represented. A handful of days after that visit, Anna died in peace—just sort of fell asleep and woke up somewhere else. Now, only weeks after bribing his doctor to let his daughters sneak him out of a rehabilitation center and home for a couple of hours to see her one last time before she passed (he told me that though she was comatose, he rolled in singing "I keep workin' my way back to you, babe," and was sure he saw her smile just a little), Anna's husband John lay weak and dependent as well. It was obvious he would soon be leaving his room to see her once again. But this time it would be for more than just an unofficial two-hour pass, the wink of a doctor's eye, and a few words from an old Four Seasons love song.

I entered his room already aware of the news that awaited me. He had been advisor, parishioner, and dear friend to me. So it was not easy to know John had been told that evening that he would not recover, and, in fact, only had days to live—maybe even hours. He was alert (he was a brilliant scientist and engineer) and thoughtful, if not pensive.

"TA DAAHH!" I sang as I slid in from behind a closed drape. He wasn't expecting me, and I wanted to make him smile.

"Well look who's here," he beamed out with the familiar New England accent that had been housed behind strong Greek features for all the adult years of his life. "Just the man I want to talk to."

And we did talk. As I knelt beside his bed, he told me of the news he had received and expressed concern whether his life had made enough of a difference. He wondered if as a man of faith he had done for others all he was capable of doing, and hoped he would hear God express approval when they finally met face to face. I assured him that he had nothing to worry about—and in so doing I realized that I had absolutely no doubt I was correct.

"I'd like it very much if you would pray with me, Art" (only "Art" sounded more like "aught" when he said it).

"It would be an honor," I replied. Then, being joined around John's bed by two of his daughters and one of his sons-in-law, I opened my mouth to pray . . . only to be ambushed by emotions I was usually able to hold in check.

We have a phrase on our pastoral team that we use to describe what we sometimes need to do in order to keep leading worship, preaching, praying, etc.—all the public things we do while our own hearts are often stirred or, as in this case, broken. We call it "going to our dishonest place." It's not actually dishonest. In fact, we always smile when we say it that way. It's just that we sometimes find it necessary to sort of fake being in control, insulate our emotions and pretend they aren't there in order to keep talking or leading our congregation without our voices cracking or snot running down our lips. I had obviously forgotten to go there while holding John's gentle, declining, noble hand that night. For instead of praying, all I could do was kiss his hand, over and over again, while sobbing over the burgeoning realization that it would never again be lifted over me in prayer or wrapped around my shoulder in greeting—at least not here on Earth.

It was one of the most unprofessional moments of my pastoral career. It was also one of the most sincere. For every tear testified to the fact that I was losing contact with someone great. I was losing a warrior. I was saying goodbye to a truly mighty man. And as I glanced over the body of a guy who was no longer strong enough to walk, had lost the ability to swallow, and had wasted away to the point of literally being skin on bone, I was aware of the fact that this was what greatness looked like. On that night, in that room, I was looking at a picture of spiritual supremacy, and I was not only starting to miss this brother who had modeled it for me, I was starting to want it for myself.

My friend died less than twenty-four hours after that visit. His last words, as reported by his daughters, were, "There she is! I see her!" and something in a language they couldn't quite make out. Then, almost as though destined to illustrate the way we treat the treasures left to us by our spiritual ancestors, I botched the announcement of his passing in church that next Sunday morning. Go figure.

Henri Nouwen, in his little book *The Selfless Way of Christ*, cautions against being caught up by appearances of religious substance that are actually little more than pseudo-religious temptations. Among those he lists are: 1) the temptation to be relevant; 2) the temptation to be spectacular; and 3) the temptation to be powerful. He didn't actually put it this way, but what Nouwen was saying was that these three overvalued traits of Christendom come with the power to lure a person not toward depth, but away from it. "Be careful," Nouwen says in so many words, "not to fill your purse with pyrite while digging for real gold. Cherish as precious what so many others are rejecting as outdated. Hold out for a sturdy, compelling spirituality and reject all invitations to anything less. Beware of shopping in a theological store full of knock-offs. The products may have the right look and a familiar label, but they'll fray at the seams after very little real use."

It's taking too long, doesn't help me to stand out right away in a crowd of my peers, sometimes appears to be moving me backward, is assaulting just about every wicked insecurity I've ever hosted, and probably isn't going to win me any "best in show" ribbons. But when it comes to the trail I choose en route to healthy spirituality, I'm longing for the one Nola and Nouwen took. I'm thinking I should follow John and Anna. Tired of the more marketable substitutes I've been choosing for too long—the faux-spirituality of boisterous faith claims and fear-based hatred baptized in Christian trappings—I'm crawling down the counterintuitive path toward the true spiritual excellence that was bequeathed to me by those who have gone before and cautioned against taking a lesser, easier way.

I'm longing to implement daily the challenge that C.S. Lewis laid down: "Die before you die. There is no chance afterward."[73]

I'm hoping you will, too—that together we can yield to the challenge of a slightly altered version of an old hymn: "Rise up, oh child of God. Have done with lesser things."

So much more easily written than done.

ENDNOTES

PREFACE

1. Church planters are people who go to places where there is no church (or no church of their denomination or sect) and start a new one from scratch.

CHAPTER 2

2. From the movie *Jerry Maguire,* spoken by the title character in reference to how difficult it is to stay on top as a sports agent.

3. Robin Maas & Gabriel O'Donnell, *Spiritual Traditions for the Contemporary Church* (Nashville: Abingdom Press, 1990), 194.

4. John Wesley, *A Plain Account of Christian Perfection* (London: Epworth Press, 1952), 100.

5. Timothy Fry, ed., *The Rule of St. Benedict* (New York: Vintage Spiritual Classics, 1981), 9.

6. Thomas A. Kempis, *The Imitation of Christ* (New York: 1952), 32.

7. Bernard of Clairvaux, *Selected Works*, 171.

8. Henry Nouwen, *Gracias* (Maryknoll, NY: Orbis Books, 1983), 162.

9. Parker Palmer, *The Courage to Teach* (San Francisco: Jossey-Bass, San Francisco, 1998), 108.

10. Dallas Willard, *Renovation of the Heart* (Colorado Springs: Navpress, 2002), 209.

11. Bill Bonner and Addison Wiggin, *Empire of Debt* (Hoboken, NJ: John Wiley and Sons, 2006).

12. Lewis Smedes, *Love Within Limits,* 33.

13. John Ortberg, *The Life You've Always Wanted* (Grand Rapids, MI: Zondervan, 2002), 112.

14. Teresa of Avila, *The Internal Castle* (New York: Paulist Press, 1979), 62.

15. Today's New International Version of the Bible.

CHAPTER 3

16. Interview by Brian Lamb, with Mark Neely Jr., Professor of History at St. Louis University and author of *Abraham Lincoln and the Promise of America: The Last Best Hope of Earth.*

17. Of course, Lincoln scholars couldn't be more split on the issue of whether he believed more than he let on about ending slavery, or was just being politically efficient for the sake of what some argue was his primary objective: the preservation of the union of states. Therefore, he's been called everything from a closet racist to "the great emancipator." If we simply take note of his major public speeches, though, a progression of thought and conviction seems to be evident.

18. Roy Bessler, *The Collected Work of Abraham Lincoln*, Volume III, 145-146.

19. Chapter 1, "The Maniac," in *Orthodoxy.*

20. Apparently even FDR was unsure of Churchill, so he sent Hopkins to England to see for himself how things stood and assess the effectiveness of the British war effort and the potential for success.

CHAPTER 4

21. This is only further complicated by the mixing of the meanings of the words "chastity" and "fidelity." In other words, some use "chastity" to refer to being sexually faithful in a marriage, while others use the word "fidelity." The point is still made that definitions are, and perhaps always have been, moving targets.

22. From an article in the December 2002 issue of *First Things* called "Celibacy in Context" by Maximos Davies.

23. Ibid.

24. For instance, in the sixth century B.C., Pythagoras oversaw a "celibate" community (meaning functionally and/or literally unmarried) because it was thought that sexual activity clouded and/or weakened the mind in some way and that seasons of abstinence promoted better and more pure thinking.

25. Gabrielle Brown, in *The New Celibacy*, talks about the growing number of people in society who find they not only no longer need or want sex, but who feel their lives and relationships (even marital relationships) have actually been enhanced by their choice to discontinue it.

CHAPTER 5

26. Smedes, *Love Within Limits,* 116.

27. Ibid.

28. Ibid.

29. Ibid, 117.

30. *The Tragedy of Pudd'nhead Wilson,* beginning of Chapter 12.

31. TNIV, Acts 6:12-14.

32. Rev. Dr. Martin Luther King Jr., *Antidotes for Fear, A Testament of Hope, The Essential Writings and Speeches of Martin Luther King, Jr.,* ed. James M. Washington (Harper-Collins: © 1986 by Coretta Scott King), 509-510.

33. Sermon by Rev. Deborah J. Blanchard, delivered at Faith Baptist Church, Littleton, CO, January 14, 2007. I am also dependent and indebted to Rev. Blanchard for her work in quoting sources for some of the MLK quotes that I have loved and repeated in this section.

34. Rev. Dr. Martin Luther King Jr., *Antidotes for Fear, A Testament of Hope, The Essential Writings and Speeches of Martin Luther King, Jr.,* ed. James M. Washington, 511.

35. Parker J. Palmer, *Let Your Life Speak* (San Francisco: Jossey-Bass, 2000), 93-94.

36. Ibid.

37. Ibid.

38. Thomas Odon, *Pastoral Theology: Essentials of Ministry* (San Francisco: HarperOne, 1983), 254-55.

39. Gregory of Nyssa, *The Life of Moses* (New York: Paulist Press, 1978), 128.

40. TNIV, I Samuel 17:34-37.

41. Ronald Rolheiser, The Holy Longing (New York: Doubleday, 1999), 116.

CHAPTER 6

42. Martin Luther, Letters of Spiritual Counsel, 266 [brackets are mine].

43. The Fray, "All At Once," from the album *How To Save a Life.*

44. TNIV, Hebrews 11:32-40.

45. Gudar, *Missional Church,* 132.

46. Francis Chan, *Crazy Love,* 124.

CHAPTER 7

47. John of the Cross, *Selected Writings*, ed. Kiern Kavanausky, 314.

48. Matthew 5:43-48.

49. Matthew 22:39, Romans 12.

50. Matthew 6:10 and John 5:30.

51. Matthew 10:39.

52. Luke 7:1-17.

53. TNIV, Luke 7.

54. Matthew 3:11-17.

55. Ibid.

56. Matthew 11:7-15.

57. Luke 1:38.

58. NASV, Luke 1:29.

59. NASV, Luke 1:38.

60. Danny Morris and Charles Olsen, *Discerning God's Will Together; A Spiritual Practice for The Church*, 17.

61. Ronald Rolheiser, *Holy Longing, The Search For a Christian Spirituality*, 123-124. His challenge is that we have freedom of choice until it becomes necessary to react to something we witness. At that point, our destiny is set, at least in the short term, by a responsibility to respond to what has crossed our path.

62. Rob is now part of our family, a dear and beloved "son" to us. He eventually moved into restaurant management, working for the same company for more than ten years, and is doing very well. He is an all-star dad, and we couldn't possibly be more proud of him or blessed by his friendship.

63. Bernard of Clairvaux, *Selected Works*, trans. G.R. Evans, 107 [brackets are mine].

64. *The Imitation of Christ*, 32.

65. John Wesley, *A Plain Account of Christian Perfection*, 5.

CHAPTER 8

66. "Michael V. Aris, 53, Dies; Scholarly Husband of Laureate," *New York Times*, March 30, 1999.

67. From USCampaignForBurma.org.

68. Ibid (italics and bold mine).

69. "Tribute to a Living Legend, Aung San Suu Kui," isikkim.com, accessed November 18, 2010.

70. Ibid (bold and italics mine).

71. From an interview by Alan Clements, circa 1996, copyrighted 1997, Gale Group. Referenced in Clements' book, *The Voice of Hope*.

72. Patrick Barata and Keith Johnson, "Washington Resumes Full Myanmar Ties," *Wall Street Journal*, January 14, 2012.

SOME FINAL THOUGHTS

73. C.S. Lewis *Till We Have Faces: A Myth Retold* (Harcourt Brace & Company, 1980).

NOTES

NOTES

NOTES

NOTES

NOTES

NOTES

NOTES